THE GATEWAY TO THE MIDDLE AGES
FRANCE AND BRITAIN

The Gateway
to the Middle Ages

FRANCE
AND BRITAIN

by Eleanor Shipley Duckett

ANN ARBOR PAPERBACKS

THE UNIVERSITY OF MICHIGAN PRESS

FIRST EDITION AS AN ANN ARBOR PAPERBACK 1961

SECOND PRINTING 1964

COPYRIGHT © BY THE UNIVERSITY OF MICHIGAN 1938

PUBLISHED IN THE UNITED STATES OF AMERICA BY

THE UNIVERSITY OF MICHIGAN PRESS AND SIMULTANEOUSLY

IN TORONTO, CANADA, BY AMBASSADOR BOOKS LIMITED

MANUFACTURED IN THE UNITED STATES OF AMERICA

TO
MARY ELLEN CHASE
AND
OUR CAMBRIDGE FAMILY
CAMBRIDGE, ENGLAND
1934–1936

ABBREVIATIONS

PL	*Patrologia Latina*
PG	*Patrologia Graeca*
M.G.H.	*Monumenta Germaniae Historica*
M.H.B.	*Monumenta Historica Britannica*
R.I.S.	*Rerum Italicarum Scriptores* (Muratori)
Script. rer. Merov.	*Scriptores Rerum Merovingicarum*
Script. rer. Lang. .	*Scriptores Rerum Langobardicarum*
C.S.H.B. . . .	*Corpus Scriptorum Historiae Byzantinae*
C.S.E.L.	*Corpus Scriptorum Ecclesiasticorum Latinorum*
P.L.M.	*Poetae Latini Minores*
P.W.	*Real-Encyclopädie,* ed. Pauly-Wissowa
C.M.H.	*Cambridge Medieval History*
H.S.C.P.	*Harvard Studies in Classical Philology*
C.P.	*Classical Philology*
Schanz	Schanz-Hosius-Krüger: *Geschichte der römischen Literatur,* IV, 2, 1920
Manitius . . .	M. Manitius: *Geschichte der lateinischen Literatur des Mittelalters,* I, 1911
Bardenhewer . .	O. Bardenhewer: *Geschichte der altkirchlichen Literatur,* V, 1932

PREFACE

THE GATEWAY TO THE MIDDLE AGES is made up of three parts. This one deals with France and Britain in the sixth century.

When the period opens, France, like Italy, is under the power of barbarian Germanic invaders of the Roman Empire. In France, however, these are Franks from the region of the Rhine.

Here, then, we follow from Latin record the story of the Frankish kings. It was Clovis who founded their line, who held great part of the land of France when he died in 511. It was he whom the Catholic Church claimed as her "first-born" among barbarians; for he turned from heathendom and heresy to submit to the Catholic Faith. Here we read of the well-known scene at Reims when its bishop, Remigius, baptized this king, with thousands of his fighting men. Henceforward Frankland was a Catholic realm in the minds of its princes, and Clovis, its founder, marched forth under the banner of his church and his state to bring other regions under his control.

Gregory of Tours, the historian of the Franks in this sixth century, is our authority for many, varied pictures of Frankish life given here, ranging from battle, murder, and cruelty unbelievable, from vice, lust, and superstition practiced by kings and queens, by hierarchy and nobles, by lay-folk of simple birth, to the high holiness of early medieval saints. At the death of Clovis his kingdom was divided into four; and we see his four sons reigning, each in his pride, at Paris and at Reims, at Soissons and at Orleans. Here in Gregory's narrative they stand out, with the long, flowing hair which was the mark of their royal birth, with tunic, breeches, and mantle of brilliant hue, armed with battle-axe, dagger, and sword, ready to use all against those who would dare to rise in their way. Their women yield nothing to them in fury of determination; the feud of two royal queens of early France, Brunhild and Fredegund, in its violence and crime born of jealous desire, fills one of the darkest pages in Frankish history.

Yet there were gentle and happy pages also. There were men of song and poetry. At the cloister of Holy Cross in Poitiers lived a Frankish priest, Fortunatus, who was chaplain to its nuns and wrote hymns for their chanting; Christian people still chant them today. He made his verses, too, for the lady foundress of Holy Cross in gratitude for offerings sent to his cell. Her name was Radegund, once a Frankish queen, and she is still honored by dedications in that name.

From France we turn to Britain and its history as Gildas the Wise told it in this time. The land of Britain, he lamented, had been swept bare by Saxon invaders. The invaders, moreover, had stayed; and Saxon occupation had driven the British to the remote wilds of the West Country, to Devon and Cornwall, and to Wales. Here reigned the Five Kings of Britain, whom Gildas held sinners of utter depravity. Yet in these remoter parts of Britain, too, lived men who cared deeply for books and their making, for such learning as their time afforded them. Here is the picture of the School of Llantwit in South Wales, where the scholar Illtyd taught youths whose names, like his, are still familiar words.

PREFACE

Gildas should not be forgotten. Much can be learned from him himself and from his medieval biographer in regard to the history and the legends, the customs and the culture, of the British of the western coasts in this sixth century, when settlers from overseas were making ready, here and there, their various kingships in the realms of what was to be known as Anglo-Saxon England.

E.S.D.

Northampton, Massachusetts, 1960

CONTENTS

THE GATEWAY TO THE MIDDLE AGES
FRANCE AND BRITAIN

CHAPTER I

A PICTURE OF FRANCE

From Ennodius, who at least as deacon in Milan could still find leisure and peace under Theodoric to enjoy the pen of a ready writer and the luxury of a mind set on words, we turn to France, to consider one whose preparation for a bishopric was entirely different. Gregory of Tours cared little for words and their ways if only he might bring some discipline and light into his little world of Gaul. He knew it tumultuous with disorder and dark with every sin, from murder, rape and robbery done by kings and commoners alike to the negligences and ignorances which were the heritage of its law-abiding and respectable citizens. There was no leisure here, save for prayer, even in his own Cathedral house. At any moment he might be summoned to pacify angry princes, quarrelling for their portions of France; to quell murderous frays in the streets of Tours; to say the last offices for those dead by violence or to give sanctuary to some fugitive flying from his doom. He never knew whether his Liturgy and his Hours in his own Cathedral would proceed uninterrupted to their end. Life in Tours under the Merovingian Kings of the sixth century was lived in the hot stir of the world's market-place, rarely relieved by some cool shadow of thought.

In Gaul there had been no Theodoric to win credit for the invader. For long its rightful inhabitants had lived seemingly unconscious of the slowly encroaching barbarian flood. The poor, bound by cruel burdens of taxation, scarcely feared the foreign settler more than their own Roman landlords. The

cultivated aristocracy had lived secure in the vain hope of
the dying Roman Empire, dying while they enjoyed its last
days on their great estates, in their episcopal sees, in their
magistracies and high places of power. Yet culture was not
extinct; writing in the fifth century had still found its votaries.
Sidonius Apollinaris and his many friends and correspondents
had still kept alive a love of Latin phrases and periods in their
elaborately turned letters and epigrams and verses flicked so
daintily from the pen. Monks of the south had fostered the
literature of religion in the island fastness of Lérins. Cassian
in his monastic instructions, Orosius in his history, Sulpicius
in his biography, had written with zeal for the souls of Roman
Christians. The priest Salvian, more aware than most, had
awakened to the presence of strange races within the Empire,
only to make comparison of Roman profligacy and greed with
the purity of barbarian character.

After these the deluge, and but a sturdy growth here and
there, scarcely rising above the fresh tide of physical vigour
that has drowned the fields of culture, will stand during the
next two centuries to show that their life is submerged rather
than dead. Not until the reign of Charles the Great will books
and their making come into their own again.

The barbarian Franks in Gaul cared, indeed, even less for
the graces of literature than did the barbarian Ostrogoths in
Italy after these had lost the impulse given by their warrior
and King. They, as we saw, had rebelled against the Roman
culture of Amalasuntha. The Franks swept on in their wild
career of acquisition, driving from their path all that stayed
them at the price of destruction far and wide. Only one force
could stem their rushing aim, and that was the Catholic
Church, when once they had been brought to her allegiance.
Not that the Church could end violence and cruelty and greed
in their hearts and hands; that were a miracle never wrought

on their free will and boisterous energy. But even for the Franks animal strength could not do all. It could conquer; but it lacked the tact, the insight, the skill and finesse needed to organize conquest into a mighty controlled realm of the Frankish Kings. Here, then, the Roman Church was to aid her convert warriors. Learned Bishops could instruct the penitents they had baptized, in ways of administration within, of civilized intercourse without. Here lay the Church's opportunity of diverting by spiritual discipline these savage sons of hers, so far as might be, from pirate raids and roving adventure to seemly work for her growth. It was thus that all unwittingly the Franks gave occasion to one of the best known narratives of these early mediaeval days.

But before we discuss this work it will be well, for the sake of clearness, to describe in a few prosaic paragraphs somewhat of the framework of this narrative, the history of the Franks in Gaul.

They were of Germanic origin, established in the third century along the lower waters of the Rhine, a loosely-knit brotherhood of independent tribes ruled by kings. Never still, always breaking forth from their settlements in search of fresh conquest, they constantly harried the Roman territory in Gaul during the third, fourth, and fifth centuries, and the great endeavour of Imperial officials was to keep them and their Teutonic neighbours, the Alamans, to their own side of the Rhine. We read of them as devastating Gaul in raids as far as Spain in the third century, even pillaging the lands of Spain and Africa. In the fourth century they captured Cologne and held it for a while till it was retaken by the Emperor Julian. Early in the fifth century they crossed the Rhine in vast numbers with the Alamans, but were driven back later on by Aetius, the general of Valentinian the third.

Yet there was no unity of cause among the Franks. Some

of them fought for Aetius against Attila the Hun; others about the same time established themselves permanently in northern Gaul with defiance of Rome. Of their number two branches stand out in prominence: the Salian Franks, who had originally dwelt on the shores of the North Sea; and the Ripuarian Franks, people of the river-bank. The earliest record we possess of their kings shows the name of Clodio, who ruled one of the Salian tribes and led his warriors to settle in the region of Tournai. He was succeeded by Merovech, one of his own family, a name surrounded by a halo of mystery and glamour. His son Childeric ruled after him, known as a loyal friend and defender of the Roman dominions.

Not so known was Childeric's son, Clovis, the founder of the empire of the Franks. At his succession to government on Childeric's death, dated in 481, he ruled but one Salian tribe; in 511, the year of his own death, all the lands of Gaul, except Burgundy and Provence, were under his control. By his defeat of the Roman general Syagrius he had gained Soissons and its neighborhood; he had thrown his power over Belgica Secunda with its chief city, Reims; he had captured Paris and extended his sway from the Somme as far as the Loire. The Alamans, who once had shared with the Franks the long course of the German Rhine, with the Thuringians and the Visigoths, had all bowed to his irresistible power.

Ostrogothic rule in Italy did impose some curb on his path. Theodoric, as we have seen, had settled the miserable survivors of the Alamans in Raetia and guarded them from the Franks' pursuing lust. We have also seen how Theodoric tried to dissuade this mighty brother-in-law from his purpose of attacking Alaric the second, the Visigothic King. After Alaric had been utterly defeated and slain by the arms of Clovis in 507 at the battle of Vouillé, Theodoric, ever seeking the peace of barbaric Europe, sent a force against the aggression of

Clovis, defeated him in 510, and seized Visigothic Provence from his grasp for Rome. At the same time he established his grandson Amalaric, son of Alaric the second and Theodoric's daughter, Arevagni, as ruler of Visigothic Septimania and Spain under his own superintending hand. But Clovis made himself supreme over both branches of the brotherhood from which he sprang: over the Salian, his own clan, and also over the Ripuarian Franks who controlled the territory of Cologne, Aachen, and Bonn. Of all the barbarian kings whose lands he coveted, only Gundobad, King of Burgundy, now remained with Theodoric to dispute his will.

The government of Clovis has left a lasting record in his codification of the Salic law of his people: the assembling, made during his last years, of the older and the latter traditions and ordinances by which the Franks were ruled. It was Clovis, also, Arian in his earlier allegiance, who glorified his name and extended his empire by bringing his people under the sway of the Church. Thus he took upon himself her wars against oppressors and heretics, carried her banner in aggressive campaigns, and in return gained the support of her prelates in his far-reaching schemes of conquest. Her "eldest son," they called him, and entrusted to him the conducting of the Council of Orleans in the year of his death. His wife Clotilda, niece of that Gundobad of Burgundy whom Clovis could not conquer, was herself a Catholic, and Clovis with ill grace endured the baptism of his sons through his wife's persistence before he gladdened Clotilda by his own submission in 496. By an irregular union he had an older son, Theodoric, and three sons through his marriage with her: Clodomir, Childebert, and Chlotar.

We may pause a moment to imagine to ourselves these Princes of the royal blood, as they are known to us from literature and relics of their civilization. They were mighty in stature and breadth of shoulders, with long flowing hair, the pride of their heritage, red or fair in colour. This they tended most carefully, parting it in front to fall on the shoulders, and allowing more of its vigorous growth on the upper lip, which alone of the face remained unshorn.[1] A close-fitting short-sleeved tunic and breeches were their ordinary dress; from a loose belt around the waist or a baldric passing over the shoulders hung the battle-axe and dagger. On festive occasions the tunic was of white or gaily coloured silk, covered by a mantle of flaming red or bright green, and above all a cloak of hides, fastened by a jewelled disc. The lower arms and the legs from ankles to beyond the knees were bare, and leather boots protected the feet. As they rode in battle-array on horses as magnificent as their riders in their trappings ablaze with precious stones they brandished in the right hand the spear; in the left they held the shield of wicker work with its iron or golden boss.[2]

Upon the death of Clovis in 511 his dominions were divided among his four sons. Theodoric, Lord of the Eastern Franks, and of the land between the Rhine and the Meuse, ruled at Reims; Clodomir governed from Orleans; Childebert made Paris his capital; Chlotar possessed the country between the Somme and the Meuse and held his court at Soissons. But no one of them was content; the fair lands of Burgundy, still unconquered, lay too near their longing eyes. These were ruled, after Gundobad's death in 516, by his son Sigismund, their mother's cousin, who had been converted to the Catholic creed and had turned with great zeal to work for his Church. The three sons of Clotilda took the field successfully against him in 523, and the defeated King was cruelly put to death

[1] Agathias: *Histories,* I, 3.
[2] See Sidonius Apollinaris, *Epistles* IV, 20, *M.G.H. Auct. Ant.* VIII, p. 70; trans. O. M. Dalton, 1915; Hodgkin, *Italy and Her Invaders,* II, p. 364.

with his entire family by Clodomir before the end of the year. The same prince with his half-brother Theodoric then marched against Godomar, a younger brother of Sigismund, and engaged him in battle at Vézéronce near Vienne. No permanent success, however, attended this expedition, as the Franks could not yet dislodge Godomar from Burgundy; and actually evil came upon them. For Clodomir was caught through a ruse of the Burgundians and slain.

Here, then, was grand chance of enrichment for Childebert and Chlotar in seizing the inheritance of this dead brother's children, and all, save one, were promptly massacred by them with this end in view. The survivor lived to become a priest and to find a place in the Church's calendar as Saint Cloud. Meanwhile Theodoric was not idle on his own account. He maintained the family reputation by conquering the realm of Thuringia and slaying its King Hermanfrid, who had taken in marriage Amalaberga, niece of Theodoric the Great. But by this year, 531, her uncle had long departed this life and his labours for peace.

The fate of Burgundy was not long postponed. At last in 534 the old ambition of Clovis found its end when Childebert and Chlotar in their hot pursuit of plunder overthrew Godomar and divided his lands among them. Henceforth Burgundy was ruled by a Frankish hand.

The same year saw the death of Theodoric, eldest heir of Clovis, and the succession of his son Theodebert, whom history describes as "exceedingly bold and eager for strife and a greedy lover of hazards." [3] In his hands the inheritance he had received from his father was safe from all attack. To him Witigis, Gothic King in Italy, yielded Provence through the fear of his struggle against Constantinople, with other lands of Gaul and a great sum of money. The distress of the Gothic

[3] Agathias, I, 4.

people was Theodebert's chance. We have seen how he invaded Italy with a vast army, wrought fearful havoc, and was only forced to retreat home to Gaul by an outbreak of plague. It was Theodebert who first among barbarian kings struck gold coins stamped with his name and likeness in imitation of Rome. He was much aggrieved because the Emperor at Constantinople, Justinian, entitled himself *Francicus*, "conqueror of the Franks," in his Imperial edicts, and he planned in vengeance a great expedition into Thrace for its conquest and after that a descent upon Constantinople itself. The story goes that a strange accident prevented him from putting this design to its proof. A wild bull, "buffalo, as I think people call it," writes a Greek historian, made a rush at him while he was hunting in his own mountain forests. Theodebert sprang aside to safety, and the animal dashed blindly on against a tree, with fatal result. One of the branches came crashing down upon the King's head, and he was found unconscious by his servants, who carried him home to die.[4]

Whether this really happened or not,[5] upon his death in 548 his lands fell to his son Theodebald, a mere boy, described, moreover, as of little spirit, without skill in war, weak in intellect and in body. He made no answer, it is true, to the demand of Justinian that he should withdraw his Frankish soldiers from Italy, where they were defending the region in the north conquered by Theodebert, his father.[6] But the Goths in Italy also remained unanswered when they called to him in their distress; for he had no mind to incur difficulties and toils of his own through the misfortunes of other people.[7] Seven years he sat feebly on his throne at Reims, and then, while he was still a lad, his life flickered out, leaving slumber-

---

[4] *ibid.*

[5] Procopius, *Hist. Wars*, VIII, 24, 6, and Gregory of Tours, *H.F.* III, 36, state that he died of sickness.

[6] Procopius, *ibid.*   [7] Agathias, I, 6.

ing embers of contention which immediately flared up between his great-uncles Childebert and Chlotar, eager for the possession of his lands. Childebert was now old and sick in body. Worse still, he had only daughters of his blood, and the Salic Law of the Franks forbade the succession of a woman, even had she been able to control their race. On the other hand, Chlotar had suffered little from advancing years. He was still sound of health, and he could boast of four sturdy sons still living from the seven that had been his, all of them as keen to enjoy their rights and riches as he had been himself. Little wonder that Childebert wisely decided to forego his claim. Shortly afterward he settled the matter by dying, and the whole empire of the Franks fell to Chlotar alone.

For three years he held it. Then, on his death in 561, division was made between these four young princes. Burgundy fell to Guntram with Orleans and Chalon-sur-Saône. Charibert gained the region round about Paris; but he died six years later, and his inheritance was parcelled out among his three brothers. Sigebert became ruler of the provinces of the Eastern Franks, called Austrasia, with Metz as chief city. He settled down there peacefully with the Princess Brunhild as his wife, a daughter of Athanagild, King of the Visigoths in Spain at this time. These three sons had the same mother. The fourth heir, Chilperic, born of another woman, inherited the region of the Western Franks about the Meuse, known as Neustria, and governed it at Soissons. He was a king of lawless ambition at home and abroad, covetous for place and wealth. His Queen Audovera he dismissed to gratify his passion for the low-born Fredegund of future fame, and then forsook her to satisfy his pride in another consort of royal blood, the Princess Galswintha, sister of Brunhild.

Galswintha was a mere girl, home-sick and frightened, as well she might be, no match for her outraged rival. Nor, indeed, was Chilperic himself, destined to reap fearful harvest of the fascination of Fredegund. The poor little Visigothic bride was speedily murdered soon after she had taken her journey from Spain to her new home in Soissons, and Fredegund reigned once more in triumph as Queen of Neustria.

But if Galswintha was of tender spirit, her sister Brunhild was not, and here begins the long story of the quest for vengeance on her part and of the restless energy of two Queens, driving their Lords into strife. The record of their reigns is full of the ebb and flow of battle. Finally in 575 Sigebert, spurred on by Brunhild, made a supreme attack upon the realm of Chilperic and gained his end. Chilperic was soon in full retreat, and the men of Neustria hailed this conqueror as King of the united Franks.

It was not likely that the Lady Fredegund would quietly submit to this victory of her rival. Again, we may think, her dark arts came into play. Sigebert fell by an assassin's hand as he was raised upon the shield, token of his supreme chieftainship, and only by stealth his little son, Childebert the second, was saved from death to carry on his name.

Now it was Brunhild's turn to play a card of revenge. Mad with pain and rage at the death of a husband she had dearly loved, she rushed to seize the first occasion. But her attempt failed, and she was carried off captive by Chilperic to live in exile at Rouen. There she succeeded where in her own home she had tried in vain, and by a quick thrust she awakened the fury of her captor and his Queen. For she cast the snare of her beauty and her spirit about Merovech, a son born to Chilperic of one of his many hours of lust and love before he had taken to wife either Galswintha or Fredegund. The two were related within the forbidden degrees as nephew and aunt by marriage, through the former union of Brunhild with the brother of Chilperic. Nevertheless Praetextatus, Bishop of

Rouen, performed the ceremony they required of him, and bridegroom and bride fled from their kin to the most holy sanctuary in France, the church of Saint Martin of Tours.

From this point another page of tragedy unrolls. Merovech escaped his father's wrath by suicide; other sons of Chilperic were killed through the vigilance of Fredegund, a stepmother true to horrid tradition, tolerant of none but the children of her own body. Yet these all died in babyhood, and when in 584 Chilperic was himself struck down by a murderer, only one little son she had borne to him remained to rule over Neustria forty-four years as Chlotar the second. Before his death he was to control in one man's grasp again all the dominions of the Franks of East and West.

Meanwhile the fortunes of the Visigothic House of Spain had been scarcely less harrowing. Here again the worker of destiny was a woman, and one as terrible in her ruthlessness as Fredegund herself. This time, however, the moving passion was not personal ambition but a religious creed. The King Athanagild, who ruled Spain from 554 till 567, had had, as we have noted, two daughters: Brunhild and Galswintha. Their mother was Goisvintha, who upheld with all the power she possessed the traditional Arianism of the Spanish royal family. After her husband's death she married his successor on the throne, a stout and valiant warrior, Leovigild by name. Both he and his son by another marriage, Hermenegild, were also loyal to the Arian faith, though the mother of this son, Theodosia, had been a Catholic and the sister of a Catholic bishop of Seville.

We can picture, then, the wrath of the older lady when her stepson wedded a Catholic girl who persistently refused to forsake allegiance to her Church. She was Ingundis, daughter of Sigebert of Austrasia and of Brunhild, and, therefore, herself a granddaughter of this Arian Queen. Her train-

ing in religion had been given her by her mother, a convert
from the Arian creed of her childhood in Spain to the Catholi-
cism traditional among the Franks since the conversion of
Clovis. Matters grew far more serious when the bride, sup-
ported by the exhortations of Leander, Bishop of Seville,
persuaded her husband Hermenegild to yield also his soul
to the keeping of the Church which both she and his own
mother loved. Bitter strife followed immediately, not only
between grandmother and granddaughter, but between father
and son; Leovigild had no intention of forsaking the tradition
of his Visigothic race. Again the struggle ended in tragedy,
the revolt of Hermenegild against his father and his death by
violence. The young widow Ingundis was committed to the
keeping of Byzantine Greeks in Spain and sent later on by
them with her little son on a far journey to Constantinople;
but she died at Carthage as she went.[8]

The news travelled slowly to reach at last her young brother
Childebert, now enthroned as King of Austrasia in his capital
city Metz, and Brunhild, the Queen-Mother, who, spirited as
ever in her second widowhood, was engaged in fighting for
her own power in his Court. The Frankish nobles of Austrasia desired a woman's dominion no more than had the
Ostrogoths before them in Italy, and Brunhild was spending
lively years. Letters were quickly sent from Metz for the
safeguarding of the child of Hermenegild and Ingundis, and
these still remain in the records of France. Two of them came
from Childebert: to the little Theodosius, son of the Emperor
Maurice, and to John, Patriarch of Constantinople. Another,
sent by Brunhild in this same year, 585, to the Empress
Anastasia, shows the human side of this Queen of masculine
energy. "My grandson," she writes, "is learning the lessons

    [8] See Gregory, *H.F.* VIII, 28. Paulus Diac. *H.L.* III, 21, has a some-
what different story. Gregory, VI, 18, represents Leovigild as pretending
conversion to some part of the Catholic creed.

of exile and captivity as an innocent babe. I beg you by the Redeemer of all nations . . . so may you never see your Theodosius dragged from you . . . do you use your power for the return of the boy and for my heart's solace in this grief. I have lost his mother, my own child; let me not lose the sweet memory which I hold of her in him." [9] But the appeals bear no fruit in our documents, and with his mother's death the little boy, Athanagild, disappears from history.

The following year Leovigild left the throne of Spain at his death to a second son, Recared, also a child of the Catholic Theodosia. In him, too, his mother's faith triumphed. He gathered a Council of Catholic and Arian bishops in 587 to debate on their conflicting creeds and then came forward himself as the leader of a great crusade for the Church, to which in consequence the whole realm of Visigothic Spain presently submitted. A few years later the King ratified his conversion by public witness before the Bishops of Spain and Gaul, assembled for the Council of Toledo under the presidency of Leander; in the same way, says the chronicler, as Constantine had appeared before at Nicaea for the refuting of the same Arian heresy. [10]

At about the same time Brunhild in Austrasia was gaining a brief triumph over the nobles ranged against her and assuring her own position behind the throne of her son, Childebert, its King. She had accomplished this largely by the aid of his uncle Guntram of Burgundy, who had formally adopted the boy as his successor. In 593, on the death of Guntram, Austrasia and Burgundy were thus reunited. Childebert, however, died in young manhood, leaving two sons, Theodebert and Theodoric, to inherit his lands. This they did by division, when Theodebert consented to rule over

[9] *Epist. Merov. et Kar. aevi,* I, pp. 149ff.
[10] John of Biclar, *Chron. Min.* II, ed. Mommsen, p. 219.

Austrasia at Metz, and Theodoric to rule over Burgundy from Orleans, and Brunhild decided for her part to rule over both these grandsons and their realms.

For some years she held her own, the more easily since her great antagonist Fredegund died shortly afterward, and Neustria, under Fredegund's young son, Chlotar the second, was no match for the power of Austrasia and Burgundy combined. But once again her dominant spirit kindled wrathful opposition, not only from the nobles of Austrasia, where she lived, but from her grandson, its King Theodebert himself. As a last resort she stirred up Theodoric of Burgundy to attack this rebellious brother, and in the struggle Theodebert was taken prisoner and killed. Now the Dowager Queen rested confidently in the hope that her rule would be secure through the sole dominion of Theodoric at both Metz and Orleans.

Her confidence was rudely broken by his early death in 613, though her ambition no reverse could tame. Immediately she proclaimed his son, her great-grandson, King of Austrasia and Burgundy combined; but this time the men of Austrasia refused to be quieted and united against her with Chlotar of Neustria. The last chapter of the life of this avenging fury among women shows her alone, captive, tormented, and finally put to a savage death.[11] We shall find, later on, that her greatness was not all of crime and violence. Her end left the King she had established powerless to maintain his throne, and in 613 Chlotar the second became ruler of Gaul in one empire of Burgundy, of Neustria and the Franks of the West, and of the Franks of the East in Austrasia.

It was, then, this tumult of life under the Franks that brought to birth one of the two works of this time in Gaul

[11] Chronicles of "Fredegarius," IV, 42, *Script. rer. Merov.* II, pp. 141f. For the influence of this great queen, as shown by the number of localities named after her in Europe, see G. Kurth, *Histoire poétique des Mérov.*, pp. 426f.

that still repay our reading. The debt which our knowledge of this period owes to Gregory, Bishop of Tours, for his *History of the Franks* is universally acknowledged. There are, indeed, chronicles which give to the historian his facts about the Merovingian age. But we are grateful to this good Bishop, not only for historical facts, but for a most vivid picture of Merovingian life in the sixth century. Kings and queens, bishops and counts, priests and nuns, saints and criminals, soldiers and citizens of every kind, play their part in this unvarnished story of humanity, painted as it is, not as it might or should be.

It is a very plain record.[12] In the preface Gregory craves pardon for any errors in grammar and at the end begs for the preservation of his narrative, despite its "rustic style." Its author was content to write as every-day men would write; for his hope was to stamp his story, not as literary, but as the work of a devout and single-hearted believer in the Creed of Nicaea. So in his opening words he declares: "I am going to write the wars of Kings with hostile nations, of martyrs against heathen, of Churches against heretics. But first I want to declare my faith, that none who reads may doubt I am a Catholic. . . . This alone is my desire: that what is to be believed within the Church I may retain with no false pretence or hesitation. For I know that by a pure faith sinners may gain mercy with our gracious Lord." Here was proper reading for simple Catholics of future days.

Gregory was in truth reared within the Church. Bishops and Senators distinguished the roll of his family; his birthplace, Clermont-Ferrand in Auvergne, was already renowned for the episcopal labours of Sidonius Apollinaris; his original name, Georgius Florentius, was changed in honour of a great-

[12] *Greg. Tur. Opera*, ed. W. Arndt and Br. Krusch, *M.G.H. Script. rer. Merov.* I; *The History of the Franks*, O. M. Dalton, I–II, 1927. See also Dill, *Roman Society in Gaul in the Merovingian Age*, 1926.

grandfather, Gregory, Bishop of Langres. His early years
were spent under the care of his uncle, Gallus, Bishop of
Clermont, and his education was directed by Avitus, Archdeacon in the same See. No wonder that he passed his days
in studying Scripture and writings of the Fathers, in admiring
the toils and triumphs related in lives of saints and martyrs,
rather than in conning pagan books for the sake of polished
culture as Sidonius had done. We are not to think that even
his religious training was deeply intellectual. Gregory's faith,
as shown in his arguments with heretics in after years, was
fervent, sound and informed, but by no means equipped for
dialectical thrust and parry. He was no Boethius. No wonder,
again, that his pious studies bore fruit, that we find him as a
boy vowing at the shrine of Saint Illidius of Clermont to seek
ordination if he recovered from the illness besetting him.
Later on we see him kneeling at the tomb of Saint Martin in
Tours, where he made a long stay in the house of Euphronius,
its Bishop. His vow was fulfilled; for he was ordained in
564 at the age of twenty-five. He was an eager, kindly youth,
we are sure, full of enthusiasm for his Church and its works,
and on the death of Eufronius the clergy and people of
Tours with one accord chose him as Chief Pastor of their
diocese. This was in 573 when Gregory was thirty-four, and
till his own death in 594 he played his part there zealously.

It was an exciting time for the land of Touraine. In Gregory's first years as Bishop its great cities, Tours and Poitiers,
so near the eyes of the rival Kings of the Eastern and of the
Western Franks, were passing back and forth as prizes of
assault in the fierce struggle of Sigebert and Chilperic. Its
lands were ravaged by armies, its streets stained with blood
of civil strife, its fields laid desolate by pestilence and flood.
The Bishop himself confesses that he grows weary of his recital
of unending trouble.

Yet light shines in its darkness. As Orosius before him, Gregory thinks it good to tell of the happiness of the true believers, together with the miseries of the unconverted: of Arius in the flames of hell, and of Hilary, defender of the Indivisible Trinity, in his native land of Paradise; of Clovis conquering heretics and spreading his dominion throughout the Gauls, and of Alaric, denier of the Church's creed, bereft of kingdom and of people, worse still, of eternal life itself.[13] In keeping with the faith of the writer there develops here a picturesque narrative of triumphs of virtue, temptation overcome and martyrdom endured, of punishment swift and sure for disbelief; of miracles, visions, portents and warnings; of crimes and horrors unbelievable piled with unsparing hand page after page; of grievous doings of clergy and nuns as well as of lay sinners. The whole flows on with a candid simplicity in a succession of stories, conversations, descriptive details, without any attempt at arrangement other than that of time, often divided year by year. Most of the record impresses us as the straight tale of one who wrote down all he believed to be true and worthy of remembrance, whether favourable or unfavourable to his cause, judged only in the light of his religious creed. Undoubtedly that light dazzled the writer's eyes occasionally, and crime in his characters is of far less import than a lack of adherence to the true Church. For his tales of marvellous happenings some one has well called him the "Herodotus of the Franks"; now and again in the earliest part he mingles fiction with history in an indiscriminate use of sources. But in the later part, where he is telling of what he himself has seen and heard, his narrative is invaluable.

The work falls thus into three divisions: the part dependent on earlier written records, the part drawn from witnesses of the incidents described, and the part which tells the events he

[13] *H.F.* III, Preface.

himself has known. The beginning deals with Biblical his-·
tory from the Creation to the days of the early Church, with
the rise of schisms and heresies, and with the line of the
Roman Emperors. Here the sources include not only the
Bible and the chronicles of Eusebius, Saint Jerome and Orosius, but also apocryphal Gospel narrative and the *Deeds of
Pilate*. Next come invasions of the barbarians and the early
history of the Franks with the succession of their kings; then
the lives and deeds of Clovis and his descendants until the
death of Theodebert, his grandson, in 548. Much of this is
drawn from the narrative of older men, together with the
writings of Orosius, and of Renatus Profuturus Frigiderius
and Sulpicius Alexander, two writers known to us through
this mention by Gregory. Here, also, we find among much
truth some tares of falsehood, as in the details concerning
Amalasuntha, daughter of Theodoric the Great.[14]

In 548 Gregory was nine years old, and for his narrative
of the years from this time, from the beginning of the fourth
book till the end of the *History* in the tenth, he relies in in-
creasing measure on his own memories, with much personal
record of his days as Bishop of Tours. The work ends in the
year 591, leaving Guntram of Burgundy friend both of his
nephew and adopted heir, Childebert, King of Austrasia, a
young man in his early twenties, and of the rival monarch,
Guntram's little nephew and godson, Chlotar the second,
King of Neustria. It leaves its story at a critical moment of
suspense, due to the conflicting aims of the two Queen-
Mothers, still alive and eager to rule supreme. Three years
later its writer was dead.

Among its varied portraits we are perhaps most grateful for
those of the Frankish princes and princesses. First, there is
Clovis, in all his ambitious energy. Gregory describes him as

[14] III, 31.

caught in peril of the Alamans, stopping in the midst of the battle to vow to Heaven his conversion in return for their conquest: "For I have called on my gods, but I find they are far from my aid. Whence I believe they have no power, these gods who do not help their servants. Now I call on Thee. I long to believe in Thee. Only, please deliver me from my adversaries!" [15] The Alamans promptly turned to flee, and Clovis was baptized, so tradition tells, by his friend the Bishop Remigius in the Cathedral of Reims on Christmas Day, 496. It was a thrilling sight. Awnings gaily decked covered the streets, white silken hangings adorned the walls of the great Church, waves of incense added their sweetness to the fragrance of wax candles flickering in the distance. How much was offered for joy of Christmas, how much for joy of Clovis? Up the nave advanced this "new Constantine," followed by three thousand of his Frankish warriors, to the Baptistery where Remigius waited to wash away the old leprosy and the stains of former years of sin. "Bow thy head in meekness, Sicambrian," he cried aloud; "adore that which thou hast burned, burn that which thou hast adored!" So was Clovis won from the graven images of heathendom. Gregory has nothing to say of the Holy Spirit descending here in form of a dove to supply the sacred oil which had been found lacking. This is the contribution of later legend.[16]

Then the King sallied out to conquer the heretics who denied the Catholic creed. So Gregory tells us: "Therefore Clovis the King said to his men: 'I am sore vexed that these Arians hold part of Gaul. Let us go with God's help and conquer them, that we may bring the land under our rule.' " With a fervent prayer he sent messengers to seek the will of God in the church of blessed Martin at Tours, for his way to battle

[15] II, 30.
[16] II, 31; *Life of St. Clotilda, Script. rer. Merov.* II, p. 344. See Dalton, II, pp. 498f.

led him thither. Just as the equerries entered the church on their quest, the antiphon pealed out: "Thou hast girded me with strength, O God, for the battle: Thou hast beaten down under me all that rose up against me." So Clovis marched forward to his campaigns, Defender of the Faith. In spite of the warning of Theodoric, the Visigoth Alaric the second was conquered and killed. The kings of the Ripuarian Franks were first bidden to get them to holy Orders, then ruthlessly slain. Cunning induced the son of the king of the Salian Franks to destroy his own father, and further cunning contrived the murder of the son. But Clovis found excuse for his deeds. He was a Catholic aggressor and those he subdued would belong henceforth to the Church's empire. Gregory does not think it amiss to declare that "the Lord daily laid low his enemies beneath his hand and increased his kingdom, because he walked in God's presence with an upright heart and did what was pleasing in His eyes." [17]

It is strange to compare with these words the last scene in his life, as Gregory himself also draws it. "When these princes were dead, Clovis received all their dominion and treasures. And when he had slain also many other kings, or their nearest relatives in fear lest they should take away his own realm, he extended his kingdom through all the Gauls. Yet to his household he is said once to have declared concerning the kinsmen whom he himself had murdered: 'Woe is me, who have remained as a stranger among a foreign people, and have no kinsfolk to aid me should trouble come.' But this," Gregory adds, "he said, not grieving for the dead, but through craftiness, pondering if he might yet find someone to kill."

The portrait of his wife Clotilda has also come down to us in mixed colours. The pious Gregory never forgets that she determined the baptism of her little sons. He tells that

[17] H.F. II, 40.

she decorated the church for the baptizing of their first-born, hoping that by the splendour of the ceremony she might win this husband whom her exhortations could not move. The baby died a week later, still in his white baptismal robes, and Clovis, as yet unregenerate, laid bitter blame on this dedication to the Christian God. We can imagine from the same *History* how eagerly Clotilda sent a secret summons to Remigius, her Bishop, when Clovis returned fresh from battle to keep his promise to the God of Victory. After his death in 511 she retired to Tours, and there "with the highest chastity and kindliness she dwelt all the days of her life, serving the church of holy Martin and seldom re-visiting Paris."

But here, again, Gregory photographed the whole picture as he knew it. He gives another story of this strong-minded woman, nursing the remembrance of past injury to her house with craving for revenge: "Queen Clotilda spoke to Clodomir and her other sons, saying: 'Let it not repent me, dearest ones, that I reared you gently. Show your wrath, I beg of you, at the wrong done to me, and avenge with wary zeal the deaths of my father and mother.'"[18] For Gundobad of Burgundy had killed his brother with the sword and had tied a stone round the neck of his brother's wife and drowned her. They were another Chilperic and his wife Caretene, parents of two daughters: Chrona, who became a nun, and this Clotilda; after their death Clotilda lived under the care of her uncle Gundobad till the King of the Franks sent to seek her in marriage. Legend has been very busy with the tale of this courting in the days since Gregory wrote. Now the sons she bore him obeyed her bidding, and the eldest, Clodomir, slew Gundobad's son Sigismund with his wife and sons and threw their bodies down a well in a village near Orleans, scoffing at

[18] III, 6.

the prophecy of the Abbot Avitus that if he slew them he and his should also be slain. But so it came to pass.

Gregory is more ready to defend the Queen-Mother in his relation of the murder of the sons of Clodomir by their uncles Childebert and Chlotar after their father had been killed by Burgundian cunning. "While Queen Clotilda was staying at Paris," he writes, "Childebert, seeing that his mother had a special affection for the sons of Clodomir, of whom I told before, was seized with jealousy and with the fear that by her support they might be given rule over their dead father's possessions. Therefore he sent messengers secretly to King Chlotar his brother, saying: 'Our mother keeps with her the sons of our brother and wishes to give them his kingdom. You must therefore go quickly to Paris and take counsel with her as to what ought to be done: whether their hair should be cut and they should thus lose their royal heritage, or whether they should be killed and the kingdom of our brother should be equally divided between us twain.' So Chlotar came to Paris, full of joy at these words; for Childebert had openly declared before the people that he and his brother king were uniting to raise the little boys to their father's throne. Now, then, they sent a message together to Queen Clotilda, who was staying at that time in the city, saying: 'Send the little boys to us that they may be raised to the throne.' Thereupon Clotilda in gladness, for she did not suspect their craft, gave the children to eat and to drink and sent them on their way, saying: 'I do not hold my son lost to me if I may see you filling his place in his kingdom.' Directly they left her they were seized and separated from their serving-men and attendants. After this was done, Childebert and Chlotar sent Arcadius, of whom I made mention above, to the Queen with a pair of scissors and a naked sword. He entered her presence and held out both toward her, saying: 'Your sons our Lords, O most glorious

Queen, seek your will regarding the boys, whether you bid
that their hair be cut in life, or their throats in death.' The
Queen was terrified by this message and exceedingly angry
when she saw the scissors and the unsheathed sword. Not
knowing what she said in the bitterness of her grief, she cried
out on impulse: 'It would be better for me, if they are not
raised to the throne, to see them dead rather than shaven!'
Thereupon the messenger, recking little of her grief or of what
she might command later after fuller thought, came quickly
with this message, saying: 'So the Queen bids, carry out your
work; for she herself desires your purpose should be fulfilled.'
Without a moment's hesitation Chlotar seized the elder boy
by the arm and dashed him to the ground; then, thrusting a
knife under his arm, he killed him cruelly. His brother heard
his scream and threw himself at Childebert's feet, seizing his
knees and sobbing out, 'Save me, kind, kind father, do not
let me die too!' Tears came into Childebert's eyes, and he
turned to Chlotar: 'Of your charity, sweet brother, grant me
his life and I will give you what you will, if only he be not
slain.' But Chlotar flew into a rage and shouted: 'Throw
him from you or surely you shall die for him. You, who began
the whole business, are you leaping so speedily from your
word?' So Childebert threw the boy to his brother, and he
caught him and slew him as he had the former, and then they
killed the serving-men and attendants, too. Afterward Chlotar took horse and departed, caring nothing for the slaying
of his nephews; but Childebert withdrew to the outskirts of
the city. Queen Clotilda laid the little bodies on a bier and
took them with sound of chants and deepest mourning to the
church of Saint Peter, where she buried them both. One was
ten years old and the other was seven."

Later on in this *History* we find Clotilda bowed all through
the night at the shrine of Saint Martin in prayer for the

averting of civil war between these two sons. And lo! a miracle. A mighty thunder-storm broke on the encampment where Childebert, the aggressor, was awaiting battle in company with his nephew, the son of Theodoric. Soon all their rampart lay in ruins. But on Chlotar, who "placed all his hope in his piety toward God," there lighted not one drop of rain or breath of tempest. "Let no one doubt that this befell the Queen's prayer through the virtue of blessed Martin." Hers was, in truth, a character in which the fierce pride of her race struggled against her Christian piety; Gregory sees her, further, as abounding in prayer and almsgiving, in all virtues. All men honoured her, he declares, not as a Queen, but as the consecrated servant of the Lord: "Neither the royal estate of her sons nor worldly ambition nor wealth brought her to dishonour, but humility bore her forth to grace."

Other Princes of the blood royal are described in the same manner of anecdote and scattered detail. There is Gundobad of Burgundy, already in Gregory's eyes a murderer again and again, who lost his soul because he dared not openly to confess the Holy Trinity but desired in vain secret baptism from his Bishop, Avitus of Vienne. There is Sigismund, his son, a convert to the Church and full of good works for its glory. But he listened to the evil jealousy of his second wife and gave order that his son Sigeric should be strangled as he lay heavy with wine after his dinner at noon. Many days the sinner spent afterwards in bitter remorse, weeping and fasting at the monastery of Saint Maurice of Agaune. He himself had established it in the Valais in honour of that martyr legion of the fourth century with whose memory legend, if not history, has associated Agaune. There, Gregory tells, Sigismund founded that "Perpetual Praise" of God in the psalter for which the Abbey was famous in later years: first in Western countries to offer its chanting constantly between the appointed Hours of prayer. It was famous, too, for another heritage of Merovingian times, its reliquary adorned with glass mosaic.[19]

Of the sons born to Clovis and Clotilda, the second one, Childebert of Paris, is shown here in a constant endeavour to wrest land from his brothers, no matter which. Now he conspires with Theodoric, now against him; now allies himself with Chlotar against their nephew Theodebert, now joins Theodebert against Chlotar; now promises to aid Chlotar's rebellious son Chramn against his father, "not remembering," as Gregory remarks, "that every time he opposed this brother Chlotar he always came off disgraced and beaten." It is Chlotar, indeed, who stands out especially among the sons of Clovis in his fierce desire of enjoyment, whether of fleshly passion or wealth or power. He was a great warrior, relentless in vengeance, even on his own kin; a man of many women, though he seems truly to have loved his captive bride, the holy Radegund who fled from her enforced union with this lord; a believer, as all his clan, in the power of the Church, though he flouted its commands and bade its clergy yield to his treasury the third part of its revenues.

Of necessity the Kings of Austrasia and Neustria, Sigebert and Chilperic, figure largely in this tale of a Bishop of Tours. Sigebert was his friend, a prince with a heart above the sordid lusts of most of the royal descendants of Clovis. Gregory tells of his marriage: "King Sigebert, seeing that his brothers took to themselves unworthy wives and even stooped to serving-women, sent envoys to Spain and sought with many gifts Brunhild, daughter of King Athanagild. For she was a maid accomplished in art, charming to look upon, upright and

---

[19] *H.F.* III, 5; *In glor. Martyr.* 74; Marius of Aventicum, *Chron. Min.* II, p. 234; Avitus of Vienne, *M.G.H. Auct. Ant.* VI, 2, pp. 145f. (for eulogy of Sigismund). See Leclercq: *Dict. d'arch. chrét. et de lit. s.v. Agaune;* Longnon, *Géographie de la Gaule au VIe siècle,* pp. 231f.

comely in character, of prudent counsel and pleasant conversation." So she seemed to Austrasia before tragedy turned all
her heart to bitterness. After this marriage we follow in a
jumbled and lively story the course of the duel between the
brothers for the possession of Touraine, till Chilperic is shut
up in defeat at Tournai, and the Franks of West as well as
East raise Sigebert on the shield at Vitry in token of reign over
them all. He, too, like Clodomir, had been warned. Germanus, Bishop of Paris, had said to him before he marched
out thence against Chilperic: "If thou shalt depart and shalt
not desire to slay thy brother, alive and victorious shalt thou
return. But if thou shalt purpose otherwise, thou shalt die.
For thus spoke the Lord through Solomon: 'The pit which
thou shalt make ready for thy brother, into that thou shalt
fall.' " And once more the prophecy came true. At the very
moment of his triumph two serving-men struck him down
with knives dipped in poison; men called them *scramasaxes*.
Who caused this murder is not surely known. Gregory declares that Queen Fredegund sent the assassins and induced
them to the deed by the strange power of her charm.

Much of history's portrait of Brunhild must be painted in
from other sources, as she lived more than twenty years after
this narrative ends. We shall find her praises in the pages of Fortunatus and of Gregory the Great. Long after her death the
Franks looked back on her as a great Queen, who fortified
their land with strong towers, ennobled it with splendid pal-
aces, opened it out by wide and lasting roads, enriched it with
fair churches. No wonder that her name passed into legend.
But in the mind of Gregory of Tours there lingers the thought
of her ruling passion for power, developed in her as the guard-
ian of the son borne to the husband she had loved so well.
At the age of five he was rescued from the death that over-
came his father; from his sixteenth year he was in her charge

as she fought and struggled for his throne. So was born that hunger for rule which drove her on to maintain her place, first as Regent, then as Queen-Mother, against the great nobles of her land, against her own grandsons, till it brought her at last to her doom. The picture is a brave and a bold one. We see her rushing to the defence of her loyal supporter, Lupus, Duke of Champagne, when he was hard pressed by her powerful enemies, Ursio and Bertefried, Dukes of her lands of Austrasia: "Vexed at the unjust attacks upon her faithful ally, she plucked up a man's courage and dashed into the conflict, crying: 'Stop, sirs, stop this evil; do not attack an innocent man; do not for one man make battle and destroy this country's hope.'" But Ursio answered her: "Retire from us, woman. Enough that thou hast held rule under thy husband. But now thy son is King and his realm is safe under our guarding, not thine. Retire from us, lest our horses trample you with the earth beneath their feet." It was this same Bertefried whom afterward she tried to save from death because she had held his daughter at the font of baptism. But he would not forsake his warring with Ursio against her and her son Childebert and was slain soon after, crushed to death on the roof of the church in which he had sought sanctuary.

Her miserable accomplice and tool, Merovech, is seen here captive of his father, King Chilperic of Neustria, submitting to tonsure and ordination as priest, then sent off to learn the duties of this calling in a Benedictine monastery. The Franks feared the mystic power of the Church, yet drove into holy Orders those whom they held unworthy to hold arms and fight as men. Later on he escaped to the protection of Tours, once again in lay dress. Gregory himself was saying Mass when the fugitive opened the door of the Cathedral church. After it was ended Merovech begged for a gift of blessed

bread.[20] The Bishop hesitated and asked counsel of his friend
Ragnemod, who had succeeded Germanus in the See of Paris
and happened to be present. Could this be granted, seeing
that Merovech had sinned by marrying his own kinswoman?
When they at last said "No," Merovech cried out so vehemently that the Bishops decided to change their minds. "For,"
Gregory goes on, "I was afraid lest by banishing one man
from the communion of the Church I might become slayer
of many. He threatened to kill certain of our people if he
had not been found worthy. Yet the region of Tours suffered many afflictions for this cause." In truth, a man in
those days might commit murder, rape, or robbery, without
qualm to himself or loss of standing among his neighbours.
But to be excluded from the pale of the Catholic Church was
to be branded among all, and the mere thought of such a
fate gave to those once admitted to its fold the uttermost
terror and disquietude. Gregory feared greatly for this impious son who said so many bitter things against his parents.
One day, we read, Merovech invited him to dinner, and as
they sat side by side begged him for a message from Holy
Scripture. The Bishop opened the Book of Proverbs and read
out the first words he happened to see: "The eye that mocketh
at his father, the ravens of the valley shall pick out." [21] "He
did not understand," Gregory comments; "but I understood
the verse as purposed by God."

Nevertheless the Bishop protected him, as one who had
sought sanctuary of the Church and holy Martin. King Chilperic sent a blustering message: "Throw out that apostate
from Saint Martin's Church or I will set fire to all your
countryside." And when Gregory wrote back that Chilperic
could not commit in Christian times a sacrilege unheard of

[20] *Eulogiae:* part of the altar bread which had not been used in the
consecration at Mass.
[21] *Prov.* XXX, 17.

in the days of heretics, the King sent his freebooters on the march to Tours immediately.

This wrath of Chilperic was vigorously fanned by Fredegund. It only ended with Merovech's order to his servingman, given when his father was hot upon his trail and the Austrasians barred him from flying for refuge to his lady of more valiant heart: "Hitherto have we both been of one soul and one mind. Suffer me not now to be given into the hands of my enemies, but take thy sword and fall upon me." When Chilperic arrived, he found his son dead. Merovech's servants were seized and punished in the Merovingian fashion. One had his hands, feet, ears and nose cut off, another was beheaded, another was tortured on the wheel, and many others, all who could be reached, were savagely put to death.

The story fits in well with the rest of Gregory's narrative of Chilperic: greedy, cruel, unscrupulous, given to all manner of bodily indulgence, desiring in his covetousness to be Lord in matters of Church as of State, victim of his passion for the evil woman he placed above himself and his people. As an enemy of Sigebert Chilperic found no favour with our Bishop of Tours, and his many deeds of violence embittered Gregory against him the more. He tells how the king worked his vengeance on lands that had sworn allegiance to his brother Sigebert; how he extended his ravages far and wide, burning churches, ruining monasteries, striking down the clergy, making mockery of convents of nuns: "There was heavier suffering at this time among the churches than under the persecution of Diocletian." Well might Gregory declare that his heart was mournful as he thought back to the time when Clovis had handed down to his sons a dominion glorious in its united whole.

It was Chilperic who ordered his doctors to tend the wounds of a man nearly slain by the hatred of Fredegund that he might endure the longer a slow torture afterward. His ambition sent envoys to Spain to seek a new bride and welcomed her with much honour and great love. Had she not brought rich treasure in her train? Soon she, like Brunhild, delighted her husband by submission to the Catholic creed; for Chilperic also combined with his evil ways a devout observance of the ritual of the Church. Once he defended himself from the wrath of his brothers by entering the debated city of Paris with many relics of divers saints carried before him for his protection. This happened on Easter Eve, and when he was safely within, he kept the Feast right joyfully, we are told, and marked it by the baptism of his son.

Yet, Catholic or not, his bride Galswintha was caught in the net of Fredegund, Chilperic's slighted consort. She begged that she might go home; she would gladly leave all her treasures behind. The King comforted her with honeyed words; but "in the end," as Gregory puts it, ordered that she be strangled, and her nurse found her one morning lying dead upon her bed. The constant harping of his evil love was too much for any compunction Chilperic may have had. He wept some tears and speedily turned to other thoughts.

But the savage deeds born of the mating of Chilperic and Fredegund must be read for their true appreciation in Gregory's own recital. Even the modern mind, undismayed by horrors real or imagined, admits a shiver at these tales of assassinations, maimings and torture. Two of them will suffice here. Gregory thus describes how King Chilperic sent his daughter Rigundis to Spain as the betrothed of Recared: "When the envoys came to fetch her, he ordered many families attached to his service to be carried off and deposited on waggons; many people who wept and refused to go he ordered to prison that he might more easily persuade them to accompany his daughter. They say that many hanged themselves in this grief and fear of separation from their relatives. Son was taken from father, mother from daughter, departing with loud wailing and maledictions. There was as great lamenting in Paris as in Egypt of old. Many people of the better class, compelled by force to leave, made their wills in favour of the Church, asking that when the girl reached Spain these papers might be opened at once, as though they were already dead and buried." [22]

The other narrative includes the story of the tyrant's death. It follows the description of this bridal journey, from which the Princess was destined to return ashamed and affronted. She left after much feasting and celebration, bearing with her all kinds of gifts from her parents and from the luckless Frankish nobles, packed in fifty waggons. Just as she passed the door of her father's palace an axle of her carriage broke, and all cried "Bad omen!" All her expenses had to be paid by the poor en route; Chilperic would allow nothing from the public treasury. Fifty of her escort rose up by night at the first halting-place and ran off to Childebert of Austrasia with plunder of a hundred horses and their golden bridles and two great platters. A whole army of soldiers went with the lady, including nobles and officials, to protect her against the marauding hand of Childebert; as they went they wrought greater havoc and seized more plunder than may be told. The land was left desolate behind their line of march. Meanwhile Chilperic, "the Nero and Herod of our time," went to his country-house at Chelles near Paris for a few days of hunting. One evening, when he had just returned from his day's sport and was about to dismount from his horse, he was struck down by an assassin, "and at once yielded up his wicked soul." "All his iniquity," Gregory continues in his short and simple sentences, "is told in my earlier narrative. He laid

[22] *H.F.* VI, 45.

waste and burned by fire very many districts, with no trace of
grief but rather of joy, like Nero in former days declaiming
tragedies among the flames of his palace. Very often he punished men unjustly to get their wealth. In his time comparatively few of the clergy attained to bishoprics. For he
was a prey to gluttony and his belly was his god. He maintained that no one was shrewder than himself. He composed
two books, apparently in imitation of Sedulius. But their feeble
little lines could not stand at all on their feet, and unwittingly
he put short syllables for long and long for short. He wrote,
too, some other little compositions, hymns and Masses, of no
earthly use. He hated the cause of the poor and constantly
blasphemed against the priests of the Lord; the bishops of
the Church were continually attacked in private by his insult-
ing quips and jests. He had different terms of abuse for each:
'frivolous,' 'haughty,' 'extravagant,' 'luxurious,' or 'con-
ceited' or 'bad-tempered.' He disliked nothing so much as the
churches. Often he used to say: 'See, our treasury remains
poor, our riches have all gone to the churches. Nobody is
King here but the bishops; our honour has perished, passed
to the bishops of the realm.' So saying he constantly destroyed
wills made in favour of the churches and trampled under foot
the instructions of his father Chlotar himself, thinking that
no one was alive to carry out Chlotar's desire. Nothing could
be imagined of lust or voluptuousness in thought which he
had not accomplished in deed. He was always seeking new
ways for harming his subjects, and if he found any guilty
men, he ordered their eyes to be torn out. So, in his instructions to the courts of law regarding his own interests, he
added: 'If anyone despises our precepts pluck out his eyes in
penalty.' He never loved anyone purely, he was loved by no
one, and when he had breathed his last all his servants deserted him."

To this picture, true, no doubt, in substance, even though
written by the friend of Chilperic's rival king, the description
of the woman who became his queen, Fredegund, makes a
more than worthy companion. In the records of Gregory she
only comes upon the scene as royal consort, replacing the murdered wife Galswintha.[23] But in another record she has
already a black page to her credit. There we read that she
was of very humble birth and maid to Chilperic's queen,
Audovera, the mother of his three sons: Theodebert, Merovech, and Clovis. Chilperic went off, the story goes, to fight
against his brother Sigebert, leaving his queen pregnant with
child. A daughter was born in his absence, and by her cunning Fredegund induced the mother herself to stand as god-
parent to the baby at her baptism. This was against the rule
of the Church, and Chilperic, already infatuated with the
beauty of her serving-woman, gladly made use of the pretext
against Audovera. The poor lady had thought to please him
on his return by this prompt lavering. But: "An unutterable
thing you have done in your simplicity," he flung at her.
"You can no longer be my wife." So he made her take the
veil in a nunnery, carrying her little daughter with her and
many estates and houses for her dowry; he sent off to exile the
bishop who had baptized the baby and he took Fredegund as
his queen.[24]

Here we have a foundation which may be reliable. On it
sober history has piled up a fearful record of crime, springing, it would seem, spontaneously from a nature almost wholly
given to evil, the more deadly in its working through the spell
of its charm. Childebert, King of Austrasia, who as son of
Brunhild was Fredegund's sworn enemy, once sent messengers to claim at Paris her surrender from King Guntram, his

uncle, to whom she had fled for protection after the murder of
Chilperic her husband. "Give up to me," he demanded, "this
murderess, who has strangled my aunt Galswintha and has
slain my father Chilperic [25] and killed with the sword my
cousins Clovis and Merovech." The susceptible and heavy-
witted Guntram, however, was fast in her toils, begging her
night after night to dine with him. So he put off the messengers
with talk of future discussion. Not long afterward one of her
secret agents tried to murder Guntram himself in church, but
was just caught in time; henceforth he, too, described her as
"enemy of God and man." She also sent more than once
minions of hers among the lower clergy to slay both Brunhild
and Childebert; and when they foolishly returned to report
failure, she maimed them with torture. To two of these she
gave knives dipped in poison, bidding them approach Childebert in the guise of beggars: "But if he is so closely guarded
that you cannot get near him, then kill her, mine enemy."
She heartened her wretched emissaries with strong cordial
till boldness rose within them, and commanded them to
take another draught to drink on the morning before
they did the deed. But her scheming was visited on them
alone.

Lesser men were equally victims of her rage. Certain Franks
at Tournai broke out into strife, and when she could not
stay their constant quarrellings with mild words she invited
them to a banquet and gave order to her henchmen to kill
three of them as they lay in drunken stupor. She detested, of
course, Praetextatus, Bishop of Rouen, because he had married her stepson Merovech to Brunhild, and she sent an assassin to kill him, also, in the place of prayer. It was Sunday,
and the Bishop was struck down while he was saying the

[25] Gregory himself does not charge Fredegund with the death of Chilperic, as another chronicler has done: *Lib. Hist. Franc.*, p. 303. Cf. *H.F.*
VII, 7 and 21; VIII, 5, and see Dalton, I, p. 122; II, pp. 562f.

psalms of the morning Office. The lady herself, a widow for now two years, was then living in Rouen, and rushed to him in pretended distress to beg that she might send her own doctors to his aid. "It is God's will," answered the dying man, "to call me from this world. As for you, who have been found foremost in these crimes, you shall be cursed in this life and God shall avenge my blood upon your head." Gregory goes on to tell that one of the Franks came to her house to rebuke her for this sacrilege: "Many wicked deeds hast thou done in this world, but never such a crime as the slaying of a priest of God." Fredegund received his words with all pleasantness. Would he not stay to dinner? When he refused, she begged him at least to take a cup of wine from the hospitality of her home. He drank the sweet draught, but it was poisoned, and crying to his companions: "Flee, unhappy men! flee from this devil, lest you also perish with me!" he fell blindly from his horse and died.

But her passion centred above all in her children. Like a tigress of the forest she burned with jealousy for them, with fury against any she might suspect of rising against them or their birthright. When she heard of the indignities suffered by her daughter Rigundis as she journeyed to that marriage with Recared of Spain which was never to take place, she ordered the messenger to be stripped of his cloak and belt and to depart instantly from her presence. The cooks and bakers and all the servants she could find who had accompanied the princess were thrashed and despoiled of their property. Later on her pride in Rigundis was overcome by hatred. Gregory tells of frequent bitter quarrels between this mother and daughter, sometimes ending in blows; once Fredegund tried to kill the girl outright by forcing her into a chest through lure of jewels inside.

Her love for her sons knew no bounds. When two of them

lay dying of the plague that raged through France, she ap-
pealed frantically to Chilperic to unite with her in making amends for past injustice, a desperate effort to propitiate
supernatural powers by any means. After their death a woman
brought her in secret a lying tale that Chilperic's son Clovis
had been its cause. He had brought it about, the whisper said,
by witchcraft learned from the mother of a girl who was his
light-of-love, one of Fredegund's own serving-maids. The
Queen's wrath, mingled with fear for the future and brooding on the dead, drove her wild for revenge. The girl was
seized, beaten, shorn of her hair, tied to a stake and planted
before the house where Clovis dwelt; the woman who had
spoken the story was burned alive. Clovis, her stepson, was
hounded to disgrace and death; his mother, the former Queen
Audovera, was murdered in her convent; his sister was forced
to become a nun, and Fredegund possessed herself of all they
had owned.[26]

Equally fierce was her wrath later on when another mis-
chievous tongue suggested that one of her sons had been
brought to his death by secret means at the bidding of an
officer of her Palace, Mummolus by name; that, moreover,
Mummolus was now boasting he possessed a remedy certain
of healthful effect in the disease which had lately carried off
her little boy. She sent for certain women suspected of deal-
ings in black arts, wrung from them confession of deeds they
doubtless never did, then sentenced them to die in various ways
of suffering, by the sword, by fire, and by the wheel. Mummolus himself, after living through torments diabolical, was
flung on a cart and thus returned to his own city of Bordeaux.
Meanwhile the bereaved mother sat at home in her grief,
gathering together every costly treasure ever lavished on this
idolized child. Jewels, toys, tunics of silk and furred coats,

[26] *H.F.* V, 39.

they filled, men said, four waggons, and she sent them all away from her sight to be burned.

Another picture of feminine cruelty is given in the action of the Arian Queen of Visigothic Spain, Goisvintha, toward Ingundis, her granddaughter and the bride of her stepson Hermenegild. Vengeance smote her wickedness in persecuting the Catholics of her country, for "a white cloud covered one of her eyes and drove from her eyelids the light already wanting to her mind." With great joy she welcomed on her arrival this daughter of her own daughter Brunhild, and immediately with kind words began to urge her toward a second ceremony, re-baptism into the Arian creed. But Ingundis, mere child of thirteen as she was, had a spirit far bolder than her years. "It is enough," she resolutely answered, "for me to have been cleansed once from sin in the baptism of grace and to have confessed the Holy Trinity in One Equality. This, I now affirm, I believe with my whole heart, and never will I draw back from this faith!" At this the enraged Queen seized the girl by the hair of her head, dashed her to the ground, kicked her repeatedly, and finally ordered the servants to throw her into a fishpond. All was in vain, and by endurance Ingundis converted her husband. He was at the time in command of Seville, and from there entered on a bitter struggle against his father the King, trusting to his Catholic supporters to defeat the Arian monarchy. At last he was imprisoned at Tarragona by order of Leovigild, and Gregory tells us that he was put to death by this same father. We shall find a similar story in Gregory the Great.[27] Another account states that he was murdered by one Sisbert, who has been held to be the officer placed by Leovigild in charge of the captive.[28] Hermenegild was canonized by the Church for his struggle

[27] *Dialogues,* III, 31.
[28] John of Biclar, *Chron. Min.* II, p. 217.

against Arianism, though there still remains against him the verdict of Gregory of Tours in this *History:* "Hermenegild, as we said above, was at enmity with his father and was dwelling in a certain city of Spain with his wife, relying on the aid of the Emperor and of Mir, King of Galicia. When he learned that his father was advancing against him with an army, he began plans for driving him back or slaying him; not knowing, unhappy man, that the judgment of Heaven was hanging over him for such purpose against his father who begot him, heretic though that father was." [29]

In contrast with so long a tale of iniquity and sorrow the character of another Frankish Saint of the Church, King Guntram of Burgundy, stands out as comparatively decent. Gregory knew him well and tells of his generosity, his piety, his justice, and his constant kindliness. He was a jolly monarch, never happier than when he was surrounded at table on some Feast Day by his friends reverend and lay, hanging on his words of jest and merriment, or when he was greeted by the admiring shouts of Syrians, Latins and even Jews, in the crowd surging about his procession through his city of Orleans. We can picture him, big of heart and slow of brain, delighting in women and wine, amiable save when affront or suspicion drove him to anger, a devout son of the Church so far as his conscience bade. Gregory tells that "good King Guntram took a serving-maid for his mistress," married a bad wife and dismissed her to marry one of her father's servants. His Frankish temper ordered the death of a royal chamberlain because some one or other had been killing bison in his forest; and once on a Sunday when he entered church for Mass, he drove away the Bishop standing at the altar to begin, declaring him a traitor and an enemy. At another time, when his wife Austrechild was dying, she declared to the

[29] *H.F.* VI, 43. His feast-day falls on April 13.

King that the doctors attending her in this last illness were to blame, and prayed him to send them with her to the grave. Guntram swore to do as she desired, and after her funeral he had both men killed with the sword, "which many wise men hold was not done without sin," observes our historian. His piety would hold no commerce with Jews, however loud their shouts of *Vivat rex*. Never, he vowed as he dined at the Bishop's Palace of Orleans, would he yield to their wicked craftiness; all they sought by their hurrahs was freedom from taxes for their synagogues, which God forbid! "O King of wondrous sagacity!" cries Gregory, differing *toto caelo* from Gregory the Great in his feeling toward their race.

But Gregory of Tours could also disapprove of this royal friend of his. Guntram at one time fell seriously ill: "It was, I think, an act of Providence, for he was planning to send many bishops into exile." Some excuse may, perhaps, be found for him. Beneath his bluff exterior there beat a heart ever in fear of the wild and savage people among whom he ruled. No more significant glimpse of Guntram can be given than that which reveals him one Sunday at Mass in Paris, surrounded by a bodyguard of armed soldiers, beseeching the congregation, men and women, not to slay him as his brothers Sigebert and Chilperic had been slain. Yet we see him at another time in Marseilles, during a visitation of pestilence, taking the lead in almsgiving and fasting and prayer, "just like a good bishop providing remedies for the healing of the scars of his people's sin." [30]

Small wonder, indeed, that anyone should be afraid in this land. From without, the Bretons were constantly making raids upon the districts of Rennes and Nantes, capturing peasants, despoiling vineyards and fields. Within, not only the Frankish Kings, but the great nobles and their servants and retainers

[30] *H.F.* VII, 8; IX, 21.

delighted in feud and brawl and bloodshed. Gregory tells of a Frankish Duke, Rauching, that he wreaked his humour on a serving-boy who was holding a candle to light his table at dinner, by ordering the candle to be pressed hard against the youth's bare legs until it went out, when it was relighted for a repetition of the torture, burning the flesh into a mass of sores. If the poor wretch cried out or jumped in his agony, a sword was flourished over his head, and his tears provoked vast mirth from his liege Lord. Another story relates that this same Duke Rauching discovered two of his serfs, man and girl, entering into wedlock without his consent. He hastened to the church and persuaded the honest-hearted priest to deliver them over to him, solemnly swearing on the altar itself that they should never be separated from one another by his act. He kept his promise by burying both alive in one grave. Yet, ruffian as he was, he feared the Church; he yielded up his prey when the priest, hastily summoned, rushed to the rescue with fiery wrath. The man was saved, but the girl was already dead.[31]

Scarcely inferior in villainy was Leudast, Count of Tours, who made Gregory's life a misery to him in his Cathedral town. His joy was to hale priests from their churches in chains, to beat other men's retainers black and blue, to rob the poor, and to desecrate even the precincts of holy Church with his lewd conduct. He was every man's enemy, and he appeared fully armed in coat of mail and helmet and lance on his official visits to the Bishop's house. Another chapter tells the savage lust of Eulalius, Count of Clermont. He began, men said, by murdering his mother. She was very pious and frequently rebuked him for his wild ways, till one morning she was found strangled in her private chapel, still wearing the hair shirt in which she used to pray. Eulalius declared his

[31] V, 3.

innocence of this deed in holy communion at the altar of his church. But Gregory has no doubt of the tale of murder and carnal wantonness fastened to his name.

Nor were the clergy spared. Much as the Franks revered the Church, her ordained representatives often met with outrage at their hands. We read of a governor of Provence under King Sigebert who seized an archdeacon at the very altar on Christmas Day, just as the Bishop was about to chant the Mass, accusing him of abetting his servants in dishonesty. He dragged the sacred minister in his alb from the Cathedral, beating and kicking him as he went, and shut him up in prison. No one, not even the Bishop himself nor the united clamour of the whole congregation, could induce him to postpone action till the archdeacon had duly honoured the Feast of our Lord's Birth. A dinner of a fish's head, poisoned by his enemies, brought death to a Bishop of Angoulême; his nephew in revenge seized property of the Church, insulted his Bishop, and tortured a priest out of life. This criminal, however, was worthily punished when he was seized with fever and his whole body burned black as a coal. "Wherefore," observes Gregory, "let all men marvel and fear to do wrong to bishops. For the Lord is the avenger of His servants." Similar stories tell of an abbot waylaid and beheaded; of a bishop assaulted by the great Duke Mummolus because he refused to support Gundobald, pretender to a share in the Frankish realm; of another bishop threatened with death by fire because he dared protect Duke Guntram-Boso, warring against the Kings Guntram and Childebert. Even the holiest places and most reverend things were not free from sacrilege. A family quarrel in Paris among men of noble rank spilled blood within the walls of holy Church; a daughter was declared by Gregory to have murdered her mother by putting poison in the cup of communion from which she drank in her Arian worship. This

story is not above suspicion, since Gregory would believe anything of Arian error. "What," he cries, "will these miserable
heretics answer when we declare that the Enemy dwells in
their sacred place?"

But his record is too sincere to whitewash even his own
erring clergy, and deeds as dreadful as those of laymen are
frankly told of them throughout his narrative. There are
shining exceptions: the saintly Germanus, Bishop of Paris;
the great-hearted Aetherius, Bishop of Lisieux; the excellent
Nicetius, Bishop of Lyons; with a goodly company of other
wise rulers of the Church, and holy monks and nuns, martyrs and ascetics. The transparent stream of the tale reflects
light and darkness impartially; but the darkness naturally
fastens itself with closer grasp upon the mind. It is gruesome
work to read of a bishop so given to avarice that he buried
alive a priest who would not yield to him a piece of land; of
two others provoking laughter at the dinner table of King
Guntram by the accusations of foul living which they threw
at one another; of another pair so confident in the name and
wealth of their episcopal estate that they "revelled with mad
fury" in every kind of crime, descending in outrage upon a
brother bishop during his birthday feast, singing and drinking in their houses all night, while their clergy recited Matins
in the church; of a priest roaming the country with a woman
dressed as a man; of an abbot slain by a wronged husband;
of claimants to a vacant See wrangling till the Cathedral was
well-nigh robbed of its furniture; of clergy plotting to remove
their bishop and falling on his official residence for wholesale
plundering when their slander had caused his arrest; of a
bishop banished from his See for conspiring against his King.

Most detailed of all is the story of the revolt in the Convent
of the Holy Cross at Poitiers after the death of Saint Radegund, its Foundress. Chrodield, one of its nuns, claiming to

be a daughter of King Charibert of Paris, rebelled against
the rule of the Lady Abbess and led a number of her sisters
in religion to break cloister and depart to Tours. Among these
was Basina, a daughter of Chilperic. "I am going," said
Chrodield, "to find my royal relatives and tell them of the
outrages heaped upon us here. We are treated in this place
like daughters of low serving-women instead of kings." "Miserable creature," Gregory comments, "forgetting the humility
of blessed Radegund!" The lady begged Gregory to protect
her sisters in the Lord, truants from their cloister, while she
herself went off to find her royal family. But Gregory read her
the letter sent to Radegund by the Bishop of Tours and six
other pontiffs, declaring the terrible punishment of excommunication for any nun who should flee her convent. So it
came about here, and after the gravest excesses on the part
of these nuns both Chrodield and Basina were deprived of
the communion of the Church by a council of Bishops assembled at Poitiers. Gregory himself was one of them. "Who
will ever be able to tell," he sighs, "all the calamities, all the
murders, all the evils of those times? Hardly a day then passed
without manslaughter, an hour without complaints, a single
moment without tears!" [32] The Lady Abbess, examined with
regard to her ruling, was found guilty of some minor irregu-
larities; she confessed to certain banquets, though such as
the Lady Radegund herself had sanctioned; to permitting
her nuns to play draughts; to allowing the Convent bath to
be used by servants. Her offences were judged venial, and
she received only a rebuke from her Fathers in God. But the
text of the episcopal condemning of Chrodield and Basina
tolls out its denunciation with vigorous solemnity.

In spite of their heinous offences both women were eventually re-admitted to communion by prayer of King Chil-

[32] X. 15.

peric. Basina, indeed, professed penitence before another
Synod of Bishops, the one held at Metz for the trial of Bishop
Egidius. Chrodield obstinately declared that she would never
re-enter her convent again as long as that same Abbess remained its ruler. She lived henceforth at Poitiers outside
enclosure in a house given her by the King, a strange reward
for sacrilege and murder.

Behind all this narrative there stands out a background of
intense consciousness of supernatural forces, common to saint
and criminal alike, fully shared by Gregory himself. Divine
retribution smites down sinners, and we can well imagine the
Bishop pointing many a moral in homely sermons to his flock.
Marvellous portents occur frequently. We are told of harvests
of strange growth; of fruit borne out of due season; of un-
canny lights flashing across the sky; of eclipses, of earth-
quakes, of sudden fires. There are other happenings still more
remarkable: water is changed into blood, drops of blood fall
from the heavens and stream from the Host at holy Mass.
Miracles abound: the sick are wondrously healed, the blind
receive their sight, prisoners and those possessed of demons
are set free. On Easter Day fountains in Spain burst forth
without agency of man, and Gregory notes with satisfaction
that when he and other bishops of Gaul differed with regard
to the date of keeping Easter from their brethren in Spain,
the Spanish waters burst forth on the day observed in Gaul!

Men also were constantly on their guard against sinister
workings of the supernatural. Wizardry was frequently de-
nounced and punished; sooth-sayers, women filled with the
unclean spirit of the Pythonic priestess, uttered their prophe-
cies through power of the Evil One. Trust must be placed,
our Bishop warns, in none and nothing but the power of God
and of His Church. Attempts at miracles by heretic clergy
are only productive of misery and confusion. Even to seek

human assistance, after having once found relief by the virtue of some saint, is fatal to the sufferer. This was learned by Leonastes, Archdeacon of Bourges, who obtained some slight aid for cataract after long prayer and fasting at the shrine of holy Martin. He actually began to see. But the happy work did not progress quickly enough, and the Archdeacon allowed a Jew to poultice his eyes, with the result of permanent blindness. So Gregory warns his readers: "He would have been cured had he not called in a Jew to aid the Divine virtue. Wherefore let every Christian take this to heart, that when he has been found worthy to receive healing from Heaven, he is not to seek assistance from human skill."

Another story forbids pride in miracles. A young novice in a monastery, of truly extraordinary zeal and humble withal, was bidden keep watch over the harvest of grain ripe in the sun. All the monks were at rest and recreation, and he alone remained on duty, when lo! a sudden storm of wind and rain. There was no time to carry his precious charge within shelter, and in his perplexity he fell to prayer. A miracle followed; for no drop of rain fell on the wheat, though the novice, prostrate in devotion, saw nothing of this wonderful work. But when he arose and learned what had occurred, he was greeted by the stern voice of his Abbot, ordering immediately a sound chastisement of stripes to be followed by solitary confinement and fasting for seven days. For: "In fear and in the service of God, my son, thou must grow in humility, not in boasting through marvels and deeds of virtue."

Such a precaution was doubtless salutary in these days when religious faith, if undisciplined, spread into weedy superstition. Consultation of the Bible for indication of one's future lot was common. Gregory tells such an incident of Chramn, son of Chlotar the first, who met his death through his own father's wrath. He seized much of Chlotar's lands and "de-

clared himself on oath his most certain enemy." The story
of his end, confused with other details, gives a good view of
Gregory's stormy narrative: "Now Chramn met his father,
but afterwards proved treacherous. When he saw he could
not escape him, he went into Brittany and there lay in hiding
with his wife and daughters and Chanao, Count of Brittany.
But Wilichar, the priest, fled for refuge to the Church of
Saint Martin. Then the holy church, because of the sins of
the people and the impious deeds of irreverence committed
there, was set on fire by Wilichar and his wife; I still sigh
when I think of it. A year before this time the city of Tours
had also been destroyed by fire, and the churches built in it
were deserted. The church of blessed Martin at the instiga-
tion of King Chlotar was covered with a tin roof and its
former elegance restored. At this time two armies of locusts
appeared, and on their way through Auvergne and the district of Limousin came to the plain of Romagnat and fought
a mighty battle there.[33] But Chlotar, raging with fury against
Chramn, marched out with his army to meet him in Brittany. Nor did he fear to go out against his father. When
both armies were lying encamped on the same plain, and
Chramn had drawn up his line with the Bretons against his
father, night came on and all remained quiet. During the
night Chanao, Count of the Bretons, said to Chramn: 'I
think it wrong that you should have to fight with your father.
Let me go out against him to-night and overthrow him with
all his army.' But Chramn would not consent, held back, as
I believe, by the grace of God. In the morning each raised his
army to action and hastened out to war. King Chlotar
marched out like a new David against his son Absalom, beating his breast and saying: 'Look down, O Lord, from Heaven
and judge my cause, how I suffer unjustly these wrongs from

[33] See Dalton's translation, *Hist. Franks*, II, p. 132.

my son. Look down, O Lord, and judge justly; bring down
on him the judgment Thou didst once bring down on Absalom
and his father.' Then they met in battle, and the Count of
the Bretons turned to flee and fell. At last Chramn also fled,
for he had ships lying ready on the coast. But he stayed to
see that his wife and daughters were safe and so was over-
taken by his father's army and carried off bound. When the
news reached King Chlotar, he ordered him to be burned by
fire together with his wife and daughters. They were all shut
up in a hut belonging to some peasant, and Chramn was
suffocated with a handkerchief as he lay stretched out on a
bench. Then the hut was set on fire above him and he
perished with his kin." [34]

There is a flavour of the Old Testament about the Bishop's
relation of belief in God and Church, mingled with such tales
of lust and vengeance. He declares that even this impious
son believed in some occult prophecy of Holy Writ. During
the struggle with his father Chramn arrived one Sunday at
the Castle of Dijon, and there the clergy placed three books on
the altar: of the Prophets, of Saint Paul, of the Gospels. Then
they prayed the Lord to show Chramn his destiny, promising,
each one of them, to read at Mass the passages on which they
should light when they opened the books. Each passage was
full of dreadful warning, and so Chramn came to his death.
In the same way Merovech, when he had fled from his father
Chilperic, placed the Books of the Psalms, of the Kings and
of the Gospels on the tomb of Martin and spent all night in
prayer, begging the Saint to reveal to him whether he would
eventually reign on his father's throne. Then for three days
he fasted and prayed before he opened the books. Each book
in this case, also, gave indication of coming doom.

Pretenders to powers of healing were numerous, and easily

[34] *H.F.* IV, 20.

found hearing. Two of them caused Gregory immense trouble; for they drew after them a multitude of the sick and credulous in his Cathedral city of Tours. One of these used such violent methods on his patients that "he either cured or killed them, and a number actually died under his torture." He wore a cowl and tunic of goat's skin, fasted in public, and stuffed himself with food so vigorously in his lodgings that his servant could not keep pace with his demands. The other rushed one morning right into the Bishop's private chapel, holding on high a crucifix, and before the startled priests could stop him began to pray aloud, alternating ejaculations to the Lord with horrible imprecations on the Lord's ministers. This same man afterward interrupted the Rogationtide procession in Paris when he tried to march with its Bishop from shrine to shrine, shouting out insults in the crowd. At last the Bishop had him arrested and ordered his pack of charms to be thrown into the river. Out tumbled a medley of roots, mole's teeth, bones of mice and talons of bears! But their owner escaped and was found dead drunk and fast asleep by Gregory himself. He happened to be visiting Paris and stumbled upon this obstacle in the dark as he was entering the church of Saint Julien at midnight to say his Office.

Relics, of course, were held in great veneration both by faithful and unfaithful. A certain Gundobald, who made much stir by declaring himself a son of Chlotar the first, though this King disowned him, and pressed a claim to Chlotar's suzerainty after the King's death, sought in support of his cause far and wide for relics of Saint Sergius Martyr. Saint Sergius, so he was told, had worked wonders for an Eastern King by his thumb. At last he heard from a friend, Bertrand, Bishop of Bordeaux, that a merchant of that town, named Eufronius, possessed some fragment from the body of

the Saint. The information was given in malice, since Eufronius had been a bitter enemy of Bertrand ever since the Bishop
had compelled him to shave his head in a tonsure, in the hope
of making him a cleric and getting possession of his wealth.
The merchant, however, had frustrated this desire by escaping
to another town and staying away till his hair had grown.
He now, naturally, refused to part with his property. Then
the Duke Mummolus, who once had served King Guntram
of Burgundy, but had deserted him for this claimant Gundobald, went in company with a deacon to seize the relics. They
were said to be hanging in a casket on the wall outside the
house of Eufronius, and the deacon managed to capture it by
climbing up a ladder, though a sudden fit of trembling almost
made him fall. Inside it there reposed in very truth a bone
from the finger of the holy martyr, which Mummolus, greatly
daring, smashed with a hammer into three pieces. But to
no avail, for all three fragments leaped into hiding and could
not be found. "It was not, I think," observes Gregory, "agree-
able to the martyr that such a man should touch them."
Honesty compels him to add that after fervent supplication
to God the fragments turned up again. But they boded no
good to their possessor.

Refusal to believe in miracles brought promptly its own
punishment, as did impiety of any kind. The judgment of
God dealt out death to the queen of Charibert, King of Paris,
excommunicated together with his wife by his Bishop, Germanus, because he had previously been united to her sister.
Another of the many wives of Charibert offered herself as
wife to Guntram after Charibert's death. He pretended to
acquiesce for the sake of the treasure she brought, then kept
the wealth, and sent the would-be queen to a convent at
Arles. Fastings and vigils were not to her liking, and she tried
to escape. But her Abbess caught her, administered grievous

chastisement, and shut her up in prison with hard labour for the rest of her life.

Heathen practices, again, were by no means extinct. Gregory tells of a visit he made to a monastery at the modern Carignan. In that district the cult of the goddess Diana was widely prevalent; so much so that a deacon of the monastery had braved all the rigours of winter, fasting on a column like Saint Simeon Stylites, and preaching to the pagan crowds of spectators below. His toil was crowned with success; for the image of Diana was crushed to powder at last, and his suffering body was healed by oil from the Church of blessed Martin.

In the matter of Church administration in Frankish times it was the King who decided who should or should not be bishop in the dioceses of his realm. Once, under Charibert of Paris, as Gregory tells, a bishop in the Province of Bordeaux was deposed by a provincial Synod of his brethren, assembled by the Metropolitan himself, on the ground of uncanonical election. But this election had been confirmed by Charibert's father, King Chlotar. The priest chosen by the Synod to replace this bishop presented himself for the royal assent; but before he could even end his short address, Charibert in a passion ordered him to be thrown out of the audience-chamber and despatched into exile on a waggon full of sharp thorns. "Dost imagine," shouted the angry monarch, "that not one of King Chlotar's sons yet lives to keep his acts? Have not these bishops driven away without our will one whom Chlotar himself chose?" The deposed prelate was at once reinstated, and the offending Metropolitan and all the bishops of his Synod were punished by fines of gold pieces according to their means. Money, it must be confessed, was always acceptable to these royal chieftains, and we read of bribes offered to the throne in support of election to holy office, a practice destined to trouble deeply the soul of Gregory the Great.

The power of the Merovingian King is revealed in Gregory's record as immense also in secular affairs. He could put his subjects to death at a word, and only rebellion on their part could make him fear. His people, however, were as bold-hearted as their sovereign. We are told that Clovis waited a whole year before he dared take his revenge upon the soldier who had dashed to pieces the holy chalice of Soissons in a fit of jealous rage. The King, though he purposed to share the booty of war with his army, had asked that this cup be reserved for him, over and above his own portion, meaning to restore it to the Church. His son, Chlotar the first, was compelled by his bloodthirsty army to fight the Saxons against his will. The ambassadors of Childebert of Austrasia to his uncle Guntram broke out into derisive laughter at this King of Burgundy in his very presence. One of them bade him not to talk so stupidly. Another, when all were leaving in anger because Guntram would not restore to Childebert certain cities held formerly by his father, threw these last words at the King: "Farewell we bid you, O King. Because you have not been willing to restore the cities of your nephew we know that the axe which cleft the heads of your brothers is still sound. Soon it will cleave your brain." Guntram in his rage ordered foul hay and mud from the streets to be flung on the heads of the departing envoys. Diplomatic courtesies were not then even matters of external form!

Though at times he must blame her clergy, Gregory ever reveals himself in this *History* as the earnest champion of the faith of his Church. We find him disputing, not subtlely but doggedly, with a Jew on the Incarnation, with an Arian from Spain on the glory of God the Son, with an erring priest on the doctrine of the Resurrection. Neither could any layman, powerful in matters of Church as the Frankish sovereigns were, dictate to him on matters of doctrine. Chilperic, a

Merovingian Henry the Eighth, used to vary his life of lusty
violence by indulging hotly in theological argument. We have
an account by Gregory of one of these struggles. "About the
same time," he writes, "King Chilperic wrote a letter to declare that the Holy Trinity should be named God alone with
no distinction of Persons. For, he maintained, it was not
proper that God should be called a 'Person,' just like a man
made of flesh. He had the document read before me and
said: 'That is what I wish both you and the other doctors
of the Church to believe.' And I answered him: 'Away with
such silly ideas, righteous King! You must follow the tradition of the doctors of the Church from the time of the
Apostles, the teaching of Hilary and Eusebius, your own confession at your baptism!' " The King lost his temper badly
during the discussion, but Gregory stoutly upheld his teachings and even told Chilperic that only a fool would follow
such a proposal.

In other ways the Bishop held his own also. As he protected
Merovech, so he boldly refused to yield up to Chilperic's
wrath the Duke Guntram-Boso, a fugitive under the protection of Saint Martin at Tours from the charge that he had
murdered Chilperic's son, Theodebert. The envoy of Chilperic stormed and threatened, destroyed Church property,
and pranced indignantly on horseback after the clergy of
Tours as they went in solemn procession from the episcopal
Cathedral to Saint Martin's Church. But Gregory remained
immovable. "Never from time immemorial," he declared,
"has such a thing been done, to deliver up from the sanctuary
a suppliant. Let the envoy fear the holiness of Saint Martin.
Did it not cure a cripple only yesterday?" The envoy's fate
came with speed. He died of jaundice, provoked by feasting
unwisely on young rabbit during the holy season of Lent.

It was Gregory alone who dared brave Queen Fredegund

and King Chilperic for the sake of justice for Praetextatus,
Bishop of Rouen, accused by them. It was he who endeav-
oured to make peace between Guntram and his nephew
Childebert, and wrote down for his readers the text of the
Treaty of Andelot in 587. We find him bearing as patiently
as he could the onslaughts of Leudast, Count of Tours, who
hated him. This man, born of a slave and in his early years
a kitchen-boy, was a minion of Chilperic. He went so far
as to declare that Gregory was accusing Queen Fredegund
of crime, and the Bishop felt constrained to say three masses
and swear solemnly at the altar that he was innocent. The
matter troubled his conscience somewhat, as saying three
masses on an ordinary day was contrary to canon, and Gregory was very particular where his ministry was concerned.
We have seen him hesitating to give the blessing of the Church
to one who was a party to an irregular marriage. It is of
interest, therefore, to read in his own record that he refused
to reconcile Count Leudast with the Church, though several
bishops recommended this, until Queen Fredegund should
recall her charges against the Count. On another occasion we
find him refusing to disobey canonical law at the request of
a fellow-Bishop, Felix of Nantes. Felix was very ill, and
wanted Gregory to consecrate his nephew as Bishop of Nantes
in his place. Gregory told the young man to obey the canons
of the Church and seek first the honour of the priesthood.
If he served diligently in this Order, in God's good time
doubtless he would rise to episcopal office.

Other glimpses of ecclesiastical procedure and ceremony
meet us frequently. A Council of Bishops in Mâcon gravely
debates whether a woman may rightly be termed *homo;* an
anchoress is enclosed with solemn chant and procession of
lighted tapers; five hundred Jews are baptized at Pentecost
outside the walls of Clermont; litanies are sung in Rome for

three days by direction of Gregory the Great in a season of
dire pestilence. Outbreaks of disease, with other visitations
of flood and famine, occur only too often in this narrative.
Once, we are told, three hundred dead bodies lay on Sunday
in the Church of Saint Peter of the region of Auvergne. Another time the fields were so full of plague that "it was a
strange thing to catch sight anywhere of a mule or a cow."
In time of famine the hungry peasants tried to live on herbs
and died. Merchants demanded exorbitant prices, and the
very poor chose slavery in return for something to eat.

At the end of the tenth and last book of his *History* Gregory
gives a list of his works with the solemn adjuration that no
one destroy, curtail, or alter them in any way. "I have written," he notes, "ten books of Histories, seven of Miracles, one
on Lives of the Fathers; I have made a Commentary on the
Psalter in one book, and one book on the Offices of the
Church." All were written by him as Bishop of Tours.

The first book on miracles describes some of those wrought
by our Lord and the Apostles and certain early confessors
and is entitled *On the Glory of Martyrs*. In the ninety-fourth
chapter Gregory relates, in what is now our earliest account,
the story of the Seven Sleepers of Ephesus, adding: "The
Passion of these men I have translated with fuller detail into
Latin with the aid of a Syrian as interpreter." This work
has now been discovered and printed by Krusch. The second
of the seven books on miracles is devoted to Saint Julian, a
martyr belonging to Gregory's own district of Auvergne. He
declares that he himself was cured of persistent headache by
this Saint's intercession, and his brother of fever. The four
books which follow tell the wonderful works of Saint Martin
of Tours, with mention of the descriptions of these miracles
written previously by Sulpicius Severus in prose, and by
Paulinus of Nola in verse. A seventh book, *On the Glory*

of Confessors, narrates the virtues and works of many saints
of Gaul who lived during or just before the time of the writer.
The one book *On the Lives of the Fathers* also deals with
recent or contemporary days.

These books are all still extant.[35] Of the *Commentary on
the Psalms* we have now only the titles of eighty-nine chap-
ters.[36] The book on the Offices of the Church has been restored
to us in a manuscript of the eighth century discovered by
Frederic Haase of Breslau in 1853 at Bamberg; its title shows
that it dealt with the calculation of the time for saying the
Offices according to the position of the stars in the sky before
dawn.[37] Titles of certain other works, also, have been connected with our Bishop, either as writer or translator or editor,
but they need not detain us here.[38]

In their language and style Gregory's writings bear the
mark of his time. Simple as they are, they are nevertheless
coloured by poetical diction in many places, by alliteration,
by plays on words, by studied phrases, by artificial arrangement. Abstract nouns replace adjectives in numerous cases,
as might be expected, and metaphors are not rare. Occasionally a Biblical phrase appears or a few reminiscences of
Vergil or Sallust. The frequent quotations from the Bible are
given, not only in the Vulgate translation, but in other rendering, probably of the Old Italian family; often Gregory
quotes from memory or adapts words to his own use. His
syntax and spelling throughout his work naturally show many

[35] Ed. Arndt and Krusch, *M.G.H. Script. rer. Merov.* I. For the story
of the Seven Sleepers, cf. *Script. rer. Merov.* VII, pp. 761ff. See, for
another list, *In Glor. Conf.* Preface.

[36] *Script. rer. Merov.* I, pp. 874ff.

[37] *De cursu stellarum ratio qualiter ad officium implendum debeat
observari.* Haase identified this MS. with the lost *De cursibus ecclesiasticis*
mentioned by Gregory himself as his work.

[38] See Bardenhewer V, p. 364. The Arndt-Krusch edition includes the
"Miracles of Saint Andrew" (ed. M. Bonnet) as the work of Gregory, but
not the "Miracles of Saint Thomas."

deviations from the classical norm. He himself pleads guilty
to rusticity, when at the beginning of his *On the Glory of
Confessors* he laments: "I am afraid that when I start writing
without education in rhetoric and grammar, cultured people
will say: 'You country bumpkin all untrained, do you expect
your name to appear among writers? Do you expect this
work to be accepted by experienced men, you who cannot
distinguish between nouns, who often mix up your genders,
who misplace your prepositions, and confuse the ablative
with the accusative? You will look like a clumsy ox in a
wrestling-school, like a crow among the doves!' At least he
knew enough to know his shortcomings, which seems to indi-
cate some training in culture. We may suspect that he could
have done better had he cared sufficiently for polish. Now
and again passages occur in which the writer has worked hard
to make his form worthy of his subject: in some story, as
in that of the slaying of Clotilda's little grandsons, or in some
outburst, as in the preface to the fifth book which mourns
the wrongs of France.[39]

The *History of the Franks* passed on as material in the
seventh century for the *Chronicles* which bear the name of
Fredegarius; for the *Liber historiae Francorum* in the eighth
century, and for the *Historia Francorum* by Aimoin of the
tenth. These, together with the *Lives* and *Passions* of saints,[40]
wove threads of legend more or less busily into Gregory's
plainer web of experience. His narrative in itself is a sad, if a
stirring one, and hints at no coming light of better days on
the horizon of this world. Its writer had not the pride of
Augustine, the anguish of Jerome, touching the earthly City

[39] See the full treatment of M. Bonnet: *Le Latin de Grégoire de Tours,*
1890.
[40] Such as the *Passio S. Sigismundi regis;* the *Vita S. Chrothildis* (St.
Clotilda); the *Vita S. Chlodovaldi* (St. Cloud); ed. Krusch, *Script. rer.
Merov.* II, pp. 329ff.

of their Empire; the barbarians were now a Christian people, and their rulers were Gregory's kings. Change and decay he saw all around him, and he was too much engrossed in recording present sorrows, in repairing immediate losses, in doing his own work day by day, to think much about the wider experiences of either Church or State outside his cure. It was enough for him to hold on to his shepherd's staff, striving to guide his people into that way of peace that still led through this earth's wilderness.

There is, perhaps, something symbolic of his life still left to us to read as we turn from the busy streets of his city into the Place Gregoire de Tours, the quiet court behind that Cathedral which stands where his once stood. Overhead little carved angels and fierce gargoyles look down from buildings of old grey stone and mortar. A tiny cloistered garden of the fifteenth century rests beside it, separated from the Cathedral by the narrow Rue de la Psallette, Street of the ancient Choir School, over which flying buttresses stretch their arms. One can still imagine Gregory passing within the doors of his Church to say his Mass morning by morning, his Office by day, his thanksgiving by night. Since his time memories of Racine and Balzac and Zola have mingled with older traditions near the Cathedral, and all has been rebuilt more than once in the lapse of centuries. But the lamps are still kindled within by the faithful who seek the intercession of blessed Martin, and one may still walk, as Gregory and his clergy walked on solemn Feast days in procession, from this Cathedral of Saint Gatien along the way of what is now the Rue Nationale and the Rue des Halles to Martin's tomb, now sheltered by a modern basilica. There countless multitudes still descend the stairs to pray before the tiny light that burns before Saint Martin's shrine. Perhaps some of them think as they pray of Gregory's tales of Clovis and of Clotilda kneeling there, of Merovech and of so many fugitives seeking its aid. Many have been grateful for Gregory's narrative of a France, if full of evil, yet also full of marvel and of mystery, of piety and strong faith, of human works of charity and things beyond human works. All, save the very blind, have smiled at its simplicity; some, recalling that interpretations still belong to God, have dared to think wistfully of a vision clearer than their own.

CHAPTER II

POETRY IN THE SIXTH CENTURY

THE word is doubtless too ambitious. Roman secular poetry died in the ancient Roman Empire with Ausonius, with Claudian, with Rutilius Namatianus, if we may add his mediocre verses. Its resurrection awaited the mediaeval days of the wandering scholars, the days of a new lyric and a new satire, ballad and hymn. Only one poet, and he is only at times worthy of the name, lies on the borderland between the old and the new: Venantius Fortunatus, of interest for his hymns and for his description of his home and its surroundings. Yet there are one or two other writers of verse whose bones we may dig up and inspire with life for a moment because they are rarely seen.

First, there is Maximian, who composed elegies on old age wretched in miseries of the present and memories of the past: five in number, with a very short epilogue. They show a return to erotic elegy, a matter in itself of some note, for it stands alone in the verse of this century. Here once more we listen to echoes of Ovid in this last of the Roman elegists. Opinions of scholars have differed very widely as to his merits. In the sixteenth century his editor, Pomponius Gauricus, boldly dared to assign his elegies to Cornelius Gallus, and thus gave him a false claim to attention. It was based on the name of one of Maximian's loves, Lycoris, and on his own story that in his youth he was of high renown in Rome, and was sent afterward on a mission of peace to the East.[1] Against

---

[1] R. Webster, ed. Maximianus, 1900, pp. 15f. See for edd. also Wernsdorf, *P.L.M.* VI, 1 (1794); Baehrens, *P.L.M.* V (1883); Petschenig, 1890.

this high praise stand dire epithets of other learned men: rake, fool, a barbarous writer, a dabbler in mud and well-nigh in filth. All scholars agree on his faults of metre, due largely, of course, to the time in which he wrote, although that Maximian had read his Latin classics well is shown by his borrowings from them.[2] Even if much of his work has truly been called an exercise in Ovid, nevertheless he brings before us a very real picture of an old man, lamenting because he can no longer live and love as he once did in the days of his prime. And, in spite of errors, the lines flow along smoothly enough for a general reader who is not over-critical. All in all, we may agree with Manitius that his poetry stands out well in his dull and dreary day of verse.[3]

There has been some dispute about his date. But he may perhaps be assigned to the middle of the sixth century on the ground of friendship with Boethius, its philosopher, which makes his greatest claim on our reading.

The first elegy begins his bitter complaint: "No longer am I the man I once was; the better part of me is dead, and only faintness and fear remain. Once I rejoiced in my powers of intellect and sensation; I was known as an orator throughout Rome. How I delighted to invent from my fertile brain those gems of rhetoric with which I adorned my speeches and won my cases in court! How I revelled in manly sports; in shooting, in wrestling, in swimming; how I loved song and dance and wine! What then was poverty to me? All I desired was mine in my perfect health and vigour. Not mine to choose my mate hastily! I walked through the city, a man desired of every girl, yet looking at none if I could not see the one ideal I cherished in my heart. She must be fair of skin, I decided, and rosy-cheeked; her long hair golden,

[2] Wernsdorf, pp. 269ff.; Manitius, *Rh. Mus.* 44 (1889), p. 543.
[3] *ibid.*

but dark her eyes. Ah me! but that was long ago. . . . *Mors est iam requies, vivere poena mihi.*

"No longer can I hear or see as once I could, no longer sing. Feebly I touch my own familiar possessions or try to find that old sweet joy in smell and taste. No more I walk to my old haunts of business or grow furious in the thrilling struggle of the Law Courts. I stand an old man, with wrinkled skin and ashen colour, with shaggy brows overhanging my sunken eyes. Gone is the jolly feast of drink and song; in its place drugs and medicines, with which I try in vain to succour my ebbing life, a shabby figure brooding alone. What purpose in careful dress, in seemly clothes, when one is old? What use in wealth for one who cannot use it? I sit as Tantalus long ago, holding for my successors what is of no comfort to me. My only occupation is with quivering lips to babble endlessly of the past. My acquaintances soon tire of the tales I tell and tell again, but I can never have enough:

O sola fortes garrulitate senes!

I laugh at my own jokes, I love to blame my own naughty self. Yes! 'wicked old dog' I cry of my own exploits in my poor little triumph, long since gone.

"Mother Earth! take back your child. Ever nearer and nearer he bows toward you; take him to his rest within your arms. My life is played, and nothing remains here for me to do. Why prolong my sorrow in all the weary round of the miseries and weaknesses of this foolish fond old age?"

So in the next, in which Maximian begs the love of his youth to remain with him in these latter years. Lycoris forsakes him now, seeking younger men; she will have nothing of his white hairs, though hers are as white as his. For she forgets the past, and heaps insults on his plea. Not so is Nature's way; birds and beasts love their old haunts and homes. Can Lycoris not love him still for what he once was to her?[4]

The fourth, fifth, and concluding poems add a few details concerning Maximian's life. In the fourth, the old man's thoughts go back to his youthful love for the dancer Candida. Her father found out his passion because he called aloud her name in his sleep. The fifth opens with the mission on which, already advanced in years, he had been sent to forward peace between the Roman Empire of the West and of the East; its date is not certain.[5] He tells us that he was of Etruscan race and that a sudden love affair with a Greek girl quenched all thought of his duty to Rome. Then the verse dribbles off into long and unsavoury laments for the impotency of an old man. The hand of Ovid is laid heavily here on the writer's pen.

The third, however, is rather refreshingly cheerful. From his store of memories Maximian calls up the thought of his boyish passion for Aquilina. He was still under tutors, she was still in her mother's care; neither tutors nor mother would favour sweet love at fifteen. Scoldings and thrashings were the only treatment meted out to the girl, but little she cared, for she was very eager for her young beloved. How could he return such devotion save by increased misery of longing on his part?

At this point a certain "Uncle Boethius" arrives. He was apparently a friend of the family and, very possibly, the author of the *Consolation* himself,[6] though gifted here with a knowledge and skill of which we should scarcely have

<hr/>

[4] See the translation by Jack Lindsay, *Medieval Latin Poets*, 1934, pp. 19ff.

[5] Wernsdorf, p. 227; F. Vogel, *Rh. Mus.* 41 (1886), p. 158.

[6] So Schanz, p. 77; Vogel, *ibid.;* F. Wilhelm, *Rh. Mus.* 62 (1907), p. 607; cf. Robinson Ellis, *A.J.P.* V, 1884, p. 2. Certain scholars have read reminiscences of the *Cons. Phil.* here and there in Maximian: see on this Wilhelm, p. 614; Webster, p. 13; Vogel, pp. 158f.

thought him capable! His sound advice to let trouble alone prevails. And so our young gentleman resolves to remain for the future fancy-free, and Boethius congratulates him on his victory over his heart. Evidently, if this picture is true, our philosopher had a merry vein of humour for his circle of friends.

Scholars have debated whether the description of the querulous old man is really a personal one of Maximian himself, or a conventional description taken from Latin comedy and erotic elegy, especially from Ovid, of the *senex*, still a prey to appetites of the flesh in spite of the infirmity of years.[7] We need not doubt that the author was versed in such descriptions and that he borrowed details from them for his use. But, surely, in spite of conventional phrases, there is too much sincerity here, the complaints are too genuine and direct, to admit of a mere objective exercise in character-drawing.[8] As we read, we cannot help pitying the sad harvest of youth that had never troubled to learn the secret of happiness for its later years. We cannot even tell whether the writer was Christian.[9] Occasionally we meet with words or lines that might well come from a Christian hand, but there is nothing to decide the point.

Maximian has left little trace on after days. Eugenius of Toledo, who died in 657, imitated the elegies in two of his lesser works;[10] and in England Robinson Ellis has pointed out two mediaeval paraphrases: one entitled "Maximon," dating from the reign of Edward the second,[11] another in a MS. belonging to the Bodleian.[12] There is also a translation by H. Walker, called *The Impotent Lover*, of the year 1689.

[7] Webster, pp. 7f.
[8] See Wilhelm, *ibid.*, pp. 601ff.
[9] Manitius, *Woch. f. kl. Phil.* 1901, p. 947; *Rh. Mus.* 44, pp. 542f.
[10] ed. Vollmer, *M.G.H. Auct. Ant.* XIV, pp. 243ff.
[11] See *Reliquiae Antiquae*, ed. T. Wright and J. O. Halliwell, vol. 1, 1845, pp. 119ff.
[12] MS. Digby 86; R. Ellis, *A.J.P.*, *ibid.*, p. 163.

The scene of the sixth century's verse now turns to Africa in the year 546 : reduced by treachery of usurpation, by Justinian's wars for its conquest, by Berber assault and military rebellion, and by the folly of Imperial government, to a state of utter misery and starvation. Ten years of alternating triumph and disaster had passed since Belisarius had contended for Justinian in Africa; at length the Emperor had sent out John Troglita, a commander worthy of the traditions of his predecessors Belisarius and Solomon. Shortly after his arrival he had defeated the Berber chief Antalas with great slaughter and had recovered Roman standards from the enemy. A second encounter with the Berbers was not so happy, and John fled, while the country around Carthage was overrun by these wild tribes seeking plunder.

The Roman commander was not daunted. He gathered the scattered forces of his own army with a host of friendly natives and allies under a loyal Berber chieftain named Cutsina, and defeated the marauders in a victory on the Plains of Cato that surpassed all hopes. "And so as many of the peoples of Africa as had survived the calamity of war, reduced to scanty number and great want, at length drew for a while a breath of relief."

Thus Procopius ends his *History of the Vandal War,* which has been no real history but only a brief summary of facts since the entry of John upon the scene. And here the poet enters, to tell of this final winning back of Africa in 548 into Justinian's Empire and of the praises of John Troglita, who has dealt this stroke of victory.

His poet's name was Flavius Cresconius Corippus, and a MS. tells us that he was a schoolmaster in Africa.[13] We can imagine how grateful he was to this soldier-hero, through

---

[13] *Opera* ed. Bekker, *C.S.H.B.* (1836) ; Partsch, *M.G.H. Auct. Ant.* III, 2 (1879) ; Petschenig (1886).

whose work he had seen the towns and fields of his land restored, made free from constant fear of attack. His narrative in verse fortunately begins where the full narrative of Procopius ends, so that we may find some interest in his details if we cannot often rejoice in his poetry. Eight books of his *Johannis* tell of the deeds of John; from the time when his name so happily occurs to Justinian as he sits grieving over the wretched state of Africa to the final triumph two years later.

As schoolmaster Corippus knew his classics, and draws on the *Aeneid* so copiously that at times we seem to be reading a Vergilian cento. There are also traces, in abundance, of Ovid and Lucan, Claudian and Juvencus. Naturally, too, the verse is correctly written. It is easy to follow, no mean boon in the sixth century, though one soon tires of this smooth imitation of real poetry.

Yet now and again passages and pictures refresh him who reads on patiently. There is the vision of the devil rising in the darkness just before dawn to terrify John as he approaches the African coast. "Thou shalt not pass!" he cries. But the soldier is constant, the fiend disappears, and John is comforted by the sight of one of God's saints, girt in a starry robe.[14] There is the picture of ravaged Africa, its cities laid desolate, its homes empty, its fields pillaged. There is the description of the enemy's camp as the messenger Amantius draws near in the moonless night, pierced by stars alone. Its blaze of camp-fires lights up to the heavens the woods and mountains all around, till stars and fires seem blended in one great burst of flame. The sentries watch while the rest of the horde of the barbarian Antalas toss restlessly in sleep, each seeing in his dream a different image of the manifold terror of war. There is the picture of John surrounded by his sol-

[14] Bekker suggests St. Cyprian of Africa: ed., p. 219.

diers, listening to the proud retort of the enemy to John's call for surrender; of John victorious, marching into Carthage in the long procession of captives, of different race and sex and colour, even of black babies held in their mothers' arms.[15]

The portrait of the Commander-in-Chief is carefully drawn. We see him grieving over Africa, full of anger at its misery; refusing to fight with Antalas till he has done all he may for the safety of captives from among his own men; boldly urging advance or inaction as the needs of the moment advise. At length the camps of John and his enemy Carcasan face each other just before the battle in the Plains of Cato. It is Sunday, and the wild natives of Africa offer slaughtered sheep to their various gods with streams of blood, with cry and shouts that ring through the heavens. Then they peer anxiously into the bodies of their victims, asking answer of victory; but every deity is silent and no words come from the minister of these dread rites. In the opposite camp all gather for Mass around the priest at the altar, prepared with the customary ritual. Then psalm and *Miserere* are heard, and the Holy Sacrifice is offered with praise and prayer and blessing.[16]

Minor sketches also stand out from time to time. The faithful Recinarius gives comfort and suggestion to John in the night of gloom, as a father to a son; Ierna, a chief of the Marmarid Languantan [17] and priest of Gurzil, carries with him in flight the image of his god; Carcasan, leader of the Syrtic people, bitterly upbraids his men in defeat, and seeks the shrine of Ammon for encouragement, where false words of the priestess send him to his death. One of the Roman generals, John the Elder, yields to temptation and flees in the midst of battle. But, as he hears the taunts of the Commander-in-Chief, he dashes back to face all odds and finally plunges

[15] I, 241ff., 323ff.; II, 414ff.; IV, 304ff.; VI, 56ff.
[16] VIII, 278ff.   [17] The tribe of Lovatah.

with his terrified horse into a deep pool of the river, safe from the pursuing enemy, from the humiliation of capture, and from the reproach of cowardice.[18]

The similes used by Corippus are worth a moment's notice. They are, of course, an imitation of earlier epic, but there is some originality in their thought and adaptation. The barbarian forces in the distance seem to the Romans like locusts carried in swarms over the land by the south wind at the end of spring. John meditates how he may save his African soldiers, held prisoners in the midst of the Berbers as wheat among thorny briars; he plays upon the minds of his men as a musician plays upon the strings of his harp. Even the familiar figure of the bees is somewhat differently applied. The General is likened to the ruler bee ordering out minions for war; like a swarm of bees the Roman soldiers alight for refreshment upon the water's edge, stooping and kneeling to drink with cupped hands or with lips bent down to the stream.[19]

At times this narrative differs slightly from the summary account of Procopius, generally, we may believe, for the worse. But historians of Africa may thank its author for the bristling names of chieftains, tribes, and places that worried so much his skill in metre, and for the descriptions of Berber warriors and customs. Corippus may be proud that he still helps to fill out a few pages of Byzantine conquest.

A second work in verse, also extant, adds little to his credit as poet, though here, also, history learns some details of interest. In this, published about 567, we find that Corippus has left his schoolmastering in Africa and is living at Constantinople. Doubtless the evil times of war had brought him to the poverty of which he complains in its Preface. It seems that Anastasius, Praetorian Prefect of Africa during the events

[18] VI, 697ff.
[19] II, 196ff., 299ff.; IV, 575ff.; I, 430ff.; VII, 336ff.

of which Corippus had told in the *Johannis,* and eagerly praised by him in that work,[20] had obtained for him some office connected with the Eastern Court, probably a secretarial post, as Anastasius was by this time Quaestor of the Palace in Constantinople. But the writer is now old and begs of Anastasius here that he will recommend him to the goodwill of the Emperor. The Emperor is Justin the second, lately enthroned in November, 565, and Corippus here gives us four books of verse, *In Praise of Justin,* commemorating the first days of his reign.[21]

The new ruler was son of Justinian's sister Vigilantia, and husband of Sophia, niece of the Empress Theodora. For years he had been closely associated with Justinian in matters of administration and at the time of his death was holding the office of Curopalates, Steward of the Imperial Palace. The names form an auspicious beginning in the eyes of Corippus: Vigilantia, Sophia, Justinus, an imposing triad of sounds.

It is night, and Justin and Sophia, asleep in their home, are suddenly aroused by loud knocking on the door. To their wrathful remonstrance the voice of the patrician Callinicus answers. His name bids good omen, and the door is opened to admit senators bringing word that Justinian has just now passed away and Justin reigns in his stead. As the royal pair pass through the sleeping city to the threshold of the Imperial Palace, suddenly all the cocks of the neighbourhood greet the dawn of this new glad day! No doubt all good citizens of Constantinople rejoiced with the cocks that the night of Justinian's last years had passed: framer of laws he had not the energy to enforce, Lord of an empire he had won back but would not rule, wringing monies upon monies from his harassed subjects to glut his ambitious ends, drowned in

[20] IV, 232ff.; VII, 199ff.
[21] For Corippus on himself see here his *Preface,* 37, 41ff. and the verses *In laudem Anastasii;* also Partsch, pp. XLIIIff.

dreams of empire and in puzzlements of theology and metaphysics.

We now wade through long descriptions of the lying in state of the late Emperor, of the funeral procession and the crowning of Justin amid the joy of his subjects in this new reign. Seven days later we find him holding magnificent audience in his Palace. Seated on his throne with its four great pillars and its awning of gold and purple drapery, under the shadow of a Winged Victory bearing a laurelled crown, and surrounded by the officials of his Court, serene among them, he listens to the complaints of the Avars, one of the hosts of barbarians in Central Europe whom Justinian had successfully subdued with the help of the Imperial Treasury. They have no desire to lose the revenue yearly accorded them in the past in return for peace, and now their chieftain Tergazis peremptorily demands this tribute as reward for defending the Empire from Thracian invaders. The answer given by Corippus to Justin must have thrilled the new Emperor's heart. Such free speaking, he calmly reminds the speaker, is not meet on the lips of those who seek audience of Rome. Think not that Rome fears you or any other people. Peace is our joy, but war holds for us no terror. To spare our subjects, to subdue the proud, is still our wont. The Empire of Rome is strong in the might of God and needs no earthly arms. Who loves peace shall find support from us; who desires war shall perish in war's disaster. Generous our hand, in truth, but not prodigal. Our troops are as the sand on the seashore, our trust lies in God, and the Avars may rest assured that we suffer no insolence from human pride. "Know, barbarians, that our fathers were victors over the Vandals, the Goths, the Alamans and the Franks. We who have subdued rulers, shall we open our doors to runaway slaves? The Lord of the Avars thinks that we fear him? Go ye and tell

him to make ready his lines and his camp. We are prepared!"

So the courtly—and hungry—poet. It is tragic to compare
with this glorious hope the cold record of history. Evagrius,
the ecclesiastical historian of this same sixth century, pictures
the dissolute and greedy life of Justin, passed in mingled
vanity and weakness till his unstable mind gave way and he
handed to Tiberius the reins of government with these pathetic
words: "Let not the splendour of thine Imperial robes lead
thee astray, nor this present magnificence, through which I
have been brought unwittingly to error and made subject to
most bitter pains. But do thou put straight my wrongdoings
and lead the State to all prosperity." It is best to think that
insanity had turned the Emperor's good purpose to evil.[22]

Our next writer wrote the worst of poems on an excellent
subject, the *Acts of the Apostles;* it deserves mention here
only for its unusual history. Its author was Arator, that pupil
of Ennodius in the school of rhetoric conducted by Deuterius
at Milan. Ennodius wrote a poem for his young friend's
birthday, of course with a play upon his name, composed two
formal addresses to mark his admission to the school and
his progress in learning, and, as we might expect, chided him
in letters for his silence.[23] We find him later on living in
Ravenna, fast friends with Ennodius' nephew Parthenius,
who induced him to read Caesar and Christian poetry.[24] But
his chief enthusiasm at this time was given to law, in which
he became a full-fledged barrister, and soon won such renown
in oratory that he was chosen by the Dalmatians as their
spokesman on the occasion of a "pomposa legatio" to Theodoric, probably in 526. Under Athalaric he went further and

[22] *Hist. Eccles.* V, c. 1, c. 13; *Gibbon,* V, pp. 16f.
[23] Ennodius, *Carm.* II, 105; cf. 114; *Dict.* 9 and 12; *Epp.* VIII, 4 and
11, IX, 1. Arator has been edited by H. J. Arnzt (1769); cf. *PL LXVIII.*
[24] *Epist. ad Parthenium,* 35ff. Three letters of Arator in verse, offering
his work to Parthenius, to the Abbot Florian and to Pope Vigilius, are
printed with the *Acts of the Apostles: PL LXVIII,* 65ff., 246ff.

gained two State offices, of Count of the Domestics and of Count of the Private Estates.[25]

But there was not much prospect of joy from official position in Ravenna after Theodoric had died. Arator was in Rome during its blockade by Witigis, begun in March, 537. At just the same time Pope Silverius was deposed by act of Theodora, and her chosen Vigilius succeeded to his place. We have a letter, written by Arator to this Pope some years afterward, in which he recalls the terror of Rome in the days of the siege and hails Vigilius as giver of liberty to the flock of Saint Peter. By this time Arator had forsaken all worldly employment and had been ordained subdeacon in the Church at Rome. But he could not forget that once as a boy he had enjoyed scribblings in verse, and one day, after much deliberation, he decided to turn his pen to sacred use in imitation of Sedulius, his favourite author.[26]

This solemn work was duly composed, dealing not with the Apostles in general, but with the deeds of Peter and of Paul, a commentary and an interpretation designed to instruct the reader in their inner and spiritual significance. The allegories and mystical explanations of Sedulius are simple compared with the elaborate parables of Arator, "plougher in the vineyard," as he loved to think himself. Two books of them, with their two thousand and odd lines, were offered, not only to his friend the Abbot Florian, to whom we have two letters from Ennodius, but to Pope Vigilius himself on the sixth of April, 544, in the presence of bishops and priests of the Church. Part of them was read on this great occasion, and their manuscript was then handed over to the secretary, Surgentius, for safe keeping among the Papal archives. But its virtue could not long be hidden. Some of the most learned men of Rome begged Surgentius that it might be read aloud

---

[25] *Variae,* VIII, 12; Manitius, I, pp. 162ff.
[26] *Epist. ad Vigilium,* Iff., 9ff., 17ff.; *ad Parthen.,* 49ff.

in public, and this was done by Arator himself in April and May of the same year.

So in the Church of Saint Peter ad Vincula a crowd gathered to listen to this praise of the first Bishop of the Church and his colleague, and under the shadow of Peter's shrine to thrill at the thought of his work all down the ages. Clergy and noble laity were there with a host of more ordinary folk, and so many were the bursts of applause and cries of "Repeat" that it took Arator four days to get to the end.[27]

No wonder that the work was renowned in the Middle Ages and was mentioned by a goodly company of writers, from the times of Venantius Fortunatus and of Paul the Deacon, who thinks Arator a *poeta mirabilis*.[28] It was a curious interest, significant of the character of these dark ages, which loved such allegories of words and numbers.

Numbers were especially fascinating to Arator, and he was forever seeing in them a mystic light. Of course, he revelled, too, in names like Felix or Aquila, which yielded a rich harvest of symbol. So, also, his joy bubbled over when he had to tell of Paul shaking off the serpent or of Eutychius falling down in sleep because Paul preached so long. Most happily it came about that he fell from the third story, for the number three was naturally Arator's special concern. Every narrative of the Old Testament, he instructed his audience, finds its mystic meaning in the New,[29] and he carefully placed the acts of the two great brethren in this light.

But alone among writers of verse in this century Venantius Fortunatus deserves more than a passing glance. And he merits far more than that: whether we recall him as the

[27] *Codex Vossianus secundus;* see preface to ed. of Arnzt.
[28] Ven. Fort. *Vita S. Martini*, 22f.; Paul. Diac. I, 25. For Arator in later days see Manitius I, pp. 166f.; M. Esposito, *Journ. Theol. Stud.* 30 (1929), p. 288; P. de Labriolle, *Dict. d'hist. et de géog. ecclés. s.v. Arator.*
[29] II, 361f.

writer of Hymns on the Holy Cross; or as the chaplain and
friend of Saint Radegund; or as the acquaintance and cor-
respondent of unnumbered men and women of his day. Kings
and Queens, Bishops and Dukes, there is hardly anyone of
importance in the history of the later sixth century to whom
Fortunatus did not address a little poem or a letter at some
time or other.

His full name was Venantius Honorius Clementianus Fortunatus, and he was born near Treviso in northern Italy, not
far from Padua.[30] We know nothing of his family except a
passing mention of a sister, Titiana, and of a brother and
nephews unnamed. In Ravenna, according to his own story,
he learned the rudiments of grammar and rhetoric and law,
which to his sorrow he tells that he forgot in later life. Paul
the Deacon was not constrained by a like modesty and wrote
an epitaph of resounding praises for the poet's tomb.[31] His
spiritual education was also duly taken in hand; for he in-
forms us that Bishop Paul (of Aquileia) "was eager for my
conversion from the time I was a child." It was, however,
some trouble with his eyes that first marked his pilgrimage to
the altars where saints of the Church are held in honour.
Both he and his friend of these days, Felix, afterward Bishop
of Treviso, were attacked by some epidemic sickness and
piously bathed their eyes in oil taken from the lamp at a
shrine of Martin of Tours in the Church of St. Paul and
St. John at Ravenna. A cure promptly followed in both cases,
and for Fortunatus the hour of destiny had struck. He must
go immediately on a pilgrimage to the shrine at Tours.[32]

This was in 565, and the young man of some thirty-odd

---

[30] *Opera poetica,* ed. Leo. *Opera pedestria,* ed. Krusch: *M.G.H. Auct.
Ant.* IV. See also *PL* LXXXVIII.
[31] *Vita S. Martini,* IV, 665 and 670; I, 29ff.; Paul Diac. *H.L.* II, 13.
See on the training of F. at Ravenna, Tardi, *Fortunat,* 1927, pp. 51ff.
[32] *Vita S. Mart.* IV, 665ff.; I, 44.

years started out to seek what in the way of adventure, temporal as well as spiritual, might befall him on his travels. In an epilogue addressed to his book at the end of his *Life of Saint Martin,* written in Gaul, he bids his little work follow backward on its way from Gaul to Italy the stages of these wanderings: from Aquileia through the country of the Veneti and over the Alps to Austria, past the waters of the Inn and the Lech to Augsburg; thence to southern Germany with leisurely course along the Danube and the Rhine. He offered prayers at every Cathedral of note as he went and begged audience of their Bishops, a hospitality which he repaid later by tributes of verse. Then he journeyed along the River Moselle to Metz, which he reached in time to take part in the rejoicing over the marriage of King Sigebert of Austrasia with the Visigothic Princess Brunhild in 566. From there he went on to Paris, very probably allowing himself a brief stay at Reims and at Soissons, to pay homage before the shrines of Saint Remigius and Saint Médard. In Paris Charibert, that King of angry passion and pride, was still ruler, though nearing the ending of his days in 567, and Germanus was its Bishop. How keenly Fortunatus was impressed by this great diocesan and his clergy we know from the poem he wrote in their praise. From this point the way was comparatively easy to Tours on the banks of the Loire.

Here Fortunatus gained his first sight of the tomb of Martin. We can still imagine his joy, even though the pilgrim now makes his way, past relics of a Church of Saint Martin built in the twelfth century, to the crypt in the modern Church on the Rue Descartes, adorned by the offerings of suppliants of latter years. The church which Fortunatus saw had been built by Perpetuus, sixth Bishop of Tours, in the fifth century. As we have noted, it had been wilfully damaged by fire at the hand of Wilichar, the priest, and restored by

King Chlotar the first. Its beauty was described by Sidonius, Bishop of Clermont and a contemporary of Perpetuus, who compared it with the Temple of Solomon, and by Gregory of Tours, who told of its fifty-two windows, its hundred and twenty pillars, and its eight doors. Fortunatus must have felt content inwardly and outwardly with the fruit of his long toil.[33]

He stayed happily a brief while with Eufronius, at this time Bishop of Tours, and then travelled south to Poitiers. King Charibert, who had been its Lord, died in the very year in which Fortunatus reached Poitiers, and we have seen the ensuing shuttlecock in which the two cities passed back and forth between Chilperic and Sigebert, rulers of the Western and of the Eastern Franks. After Chilperic was killed in 584, his brother Guntram of Burgundy tried to seize both. But their burghers decided to be ruled by Childebert, Sigebert's son and successor. Once more strife and havoc ravaged the land, till in desperation both submitted to Guntram, though Poitiers soon broke its forced allegiance and had to be reduced to submission again by repeated vengeance, wreaked on all the region of Poitou.

But the calamities of Poitou and Touraine while Fortunatus lived within their boundaries, from 567 onward, may be read in the pages of Gregory of Tours. Nothing among them seems to have disturbed overmuch the calm tenor of the life to which the pilgrim soon settled down. Two events decided its course: he was ordained priest, and he was introduced to the Lady Radegund shortly after she had founded the Convent of the Holy Cross in Poitiers. A friendship quickly ripened, and soon we find our priest established within the peaceful shelter of this Order of pious women, where for twenty years he was to lead that life of curiously mingled spirituality and

[33] Sidonius, *Letters*, IV, 18; Greg. Tur. *H.F.* II, 14; IV, 20; X, 31.

frank enjoyment of the pleasant things of this world which
made of him, at least for us, the earliest poet of mediaeval
Gaul.

The royal Lady Radegund had come to monastic peace
from great tribulation.[34] Her father, King Berthar, had
shared the rule of Thuringia with his two brothers and had
been killed by one of them, Hermanfrid. The story runs in
Gregory's narrative that Hermanfrid's wife, Amalaberga, was
bitterly resentful of the divided power and was constantly
urging her husband to enlarge his own portion. One day,
when the King came home for dinner, he found only half of
the table made ready for the meal. "What means this?" he
asked. "He who is despoiled from the midst of his kingdom,"
was his Queen's reply, "needs must have his table bare to
the midst." Such retorts after a while became wearisome,
and Hermanfrid invited Theodoric of the Franks, son of
Clovis, to march with him against Berthar, promising him
an equal share of the spoil. The campaign was successful,
Berthar was slain, and the orphaned little girl Radegund
passed to the care of her victorious uncle.

But the promise he had made was not carried out; Theodoric did not receive his share and determined on revenge.
He made a like offer, this time to his brother Chlotar, and
summoned his own Frankish warriors to march against the
faithless Hermanfrid, painting in vigorous words for them
the wrongs done to the Franks by Thuringian princes. They
were easily persuaded to follow him for plunder. "Let us go
forth with God's help against them," cried the Frankish King
at the end of his harangue, and all shouted assent. Hermanfrid was defeated with great loss, and the girl princess, once
more a captive, fell by casting of lots to Chlotar. She was

---

[34] For her see *Vitae S. Radegundis libri duo:* I (by Fortunatus), II (by
the nun Baudonivia) : ed. Krusch, *Script. rer. Merov.* II.

still but a child and he sent her to his country house of Athies, near the River Somme in the district of Saint Quentin. There, be it said to his credit, she was carefully trained, not only to understand the directing of household duties, but to read books and to care for literature. For Chlotar was eager to make her his queen and was really very proud of his attractive young prisoner. Already, however, the charm of a life devoted to the cloister was calling her, and when the King made plans in earnest for their union, she ran away from Athies after nightfall with two or three of her servants. But soon she was found and brought back for the marriage with Chlotar in his capital of Soissons.

From this time she lived in his Palace near the city, as, he soon complained, rather like a nun than like a queen. She spent her days, obedient to the priests who directed her practice of religion, in prayer and fasting and works of charity. A tenth of her money was given to the Church in alms; King Chlotar was generous in his love and her funds were plentiful. We read that she was able to found a house of shelter for needy women at Athies. Nor did she only give money to the poor people at her door. She washed and tended them with her own hands, stole out in the dark with her servants, winter or summer, to help the suffering, and gladly aided with food and shelter all the travelling monks and friars who might cheer her in their turn with words of counsel. Whenever she could escape the King's vigilant eye, her biographer relates, she dined on lentils or beans like the Three Children. All Lent she wore a tunic of haircloth under her splendid robes; and frequently in order to say her office she would steal away in the evenings from the royal banqueting table or from the royal bedchamber in the middle of the night.

Such a life with her Frankish husband could only be very difficult, and at last it became unbearable. For some reason

unknown Chlotar caused the death of the Queen's brother,
whom she loved the more because he had shared her escape
from perils in Thuringia. She then fled the Court at Soissons
and reached Noyon, where on her knees she begged its Bishop,
Médard, to dedicate her to a life of religious rule. Médard
hesitated, as well he might; not because she was the wife of
the great Chlotar of terrific power and passion, and certain
men of noble rank were even then trying to drag the Bishop
from the altar to prevent this cloistering of their Queen, but
because she was already bound by vows of marriage. Radegund, however, was firm. Leaving the distressed prelate, she
hastened to the sanctuary of his Cathedral, dressed herself in
religious habit, and again appeared before him at his altar:
"If thou shalt delay to consecrate me," she cried, "and shalt
fear man rather than God, the soul of this thy sheep shall be
required of thy hand, O shepherd!"

The thunder of this argument, we are told, quieted the
reluctance of Médard; though Chlotar, apparently, had not
yet shown his willingness to part from his queen, and
certainly showed no desire to enter a monastery on his own
part. *Locus sane lubricus ac difficilis,* as Mabillon well puts it,
for future Churchmen to judge, [35] and Médard was canonized
by the Church for his holiness. It was a formidable thing in
those days to refuse monastic retreat to a soul that craved it,
and certainly Radegund's union with Chlotar, man of many
loves, was a mockery of married life. The Bishop laid his
hands upon her and set her apart from the world; she seems
to have hurried off from her Palace so quickly that she was
still wearing her Queen's array. This she now laid upon the
altar and gave her golden girdle to the poor.

Then, after a brief visit to the shrine of Martin of Tours,
she retired to prepare for the future and lived in retreat for a

[35] *Annales Bened.* I, p. 124.

while on an estate of Chlotar's own gift to her near Poitiers, probably the modern Saix. It was through the generosity of this same discarded husband that she was able to found her Convent in Poitiers. He had set out to recapture her and had actually reached Tours, when he was met by the intercession of Germanus, Bishop of Paris, to whom Radegund had turned for help in the terror of this news. Only Germanus could bring Chlotar to realize the wrong he had done to the child he had bereaved and the girl he had married against her will. The King showed his penitence by the gift of the Convent and its endowing, and left Radegund for the rest of time to the course of her own choice.

In Poitiers, then, about 560, Radegund dedicated herself to permanent enclosure and received the aspirants who soon flocked to join her order. For its Rule she went to Arles and chose that drawn up in this same century by Caesarius, its Bishop, for the nuns living under the governing of his sister, the Lady Abbess Caesaria; [36] with the concurrence of her own sister-nuns she appointed one of their number, Agnes by name, as their first Abbess. The direction of the Community fell by proper right to the Bishop of Poitiers, one Maroveus at this time. But he did not approve of Radegund and her monastic founding, and she was obliged, as we shall see, to have recourse to the Bishop of Tours when she needed a Bishop's aid. Chlotar gave her secular protection while he lived, and after his death she placed her nuns under the care of his son, Sigebert of Austrasia. Her devoted forethought went even further, and letters to her other stepsons, Charibert, Guntram, and Chilperic, brought from them in answer their sworn witness to the endowment she had made. Finally, to the Bishops of some of the chief Sees in France she addressed another letter, still to be read in the

[36] Greg. Tur. *H.F.* IX, 42; Ven. Fort. *Carm.* VIII, 3, 47ff.; *Vita Radeg.*

pages of Gregory's *History*, telling these Fathers in God what she had done and begging their protection for her Convent, her Order, and its Rule and property. We have also a letter written to Radegund by seven of Gaul's leading Bishops, without, however, the Bishop of Poitiers, enjoining permanence of cloister within its walls, under the extreme penalty of excommunication. [37]

We do not know exactly how the friendship first began between the chief actors in our story of Holy Cross at Poitiers: Fortunatus, Radegund, and Agnes. Possibly Fortunatus was recommended to the nuns by one of the bishops whom Radegund had known as Queen; perhaps by Germanus of Paris, whose word would be sufficient for her in her veneration of his holy life. [38] It is not difficult to understand the intimacy and affection which grew up between the three. Here for Radegund was a friend of cultured taste, in constant touch with movements secular and spiritual. She must have longed for conversation on books and other things of intellectual interest, all too rare, we may imagine, for a cloistered nun of these times. Many of her Community were, doubtless, of noble rank; but probably few had been educated, as she had been in Athies, to love reading and talk along literary paths. Here, too, was one whom the Sisters could send forth to represent them in case of need, of whom they could rightly be proud, who would ably defend their interests in the midst of discord and suspicion. It was pleasant to have dwelling near them in the Chaplain's House a man to whose spiritual power as priest, to whose gifts as student and writer, to whose social attractiveness within and without their Convent, Radegund and her sisters in their

---

[37] *H.F.* IX, 42 and 39. See also Radegund's will in Pertz, *Diplomata*, I, pp. 8ff.

[38] R. Koebner, *Beitr. zur Kulturgesch. d. Mittelalters*, XXII, 1915, p. 42. Fortunatus says of himself: *Martinum cupiens voto Radegundis adhaesi: Carm.* VIII, 1, 21.

humility could pay a deference urged both by inclination and by conscience. It was pleasant, no doubt, to find in this gifted man one who delightfully and gratefully accepted the little marks of affection and hospitality which so often travelled from the Convent to his house and added their own joy and interest to the donors and devisers. Radegund and Agnes were true women as well as nuns!

On the side of Fortunatus the friendship was equally inno-cent, if his life was not as heroic. He, also, was humble, and never dreamed of aiming at the spiritual heights he admired so greatly in Radegund. He was content to follow in the beaten ways of his office as priest, ministering of his power to these devoted women within the Convent, often serving them by laborious errands and momentous interviews in the world with-out, at real cost to his natural enjoyment of calm and pleasant days. It was not his business, he realized, to follow Radegund and her more ambitious sisters in their desire for higher austerity and deeper solitude. Enough for him to praise their merits, to be ready with counsels spiritual and practical, and to proffer with sincere feeling his gratitude for the ministrations so happily rendered in return for his own. The peaceful round of religious exercises, of hours spent in his writing of poetry, in correspondence with a host of acquaintances outside, in inter-change of talk or notes or gifts with his friends within the enclosure, varied by many journeys through Gaul, held him a willing captive for twenty years. These years bore much fruit in manuscript: eleven books of poems, mostly in elegiacs, vary-ing from a few lines to some four hundred; an appendix con-taining some thirty more ranked as genuine; [39] a *Life of Saint Martin* in four books of hexameters; also, in prose, some letters, a commentary on the Lord's Prayer, another on the Apostles' Creed, and brief *Lives* of certain saints, including the Found-

[39] Leo, ed. p. VIII; pp. 271ff.

ress of Holy Cross herself. From this *Life* and from one written
to supplement it by Baudonivia, one of the nuns in this
enclosure, we gain our picture of Radegund, filled out by many
poems of Fortunatus and by the work of Gregory of Tours.

To his friends in high station, both ecclesiastic and secular,
Fortunatus writes of the marvels they are building, of the great
houses which are their homes and in which he has been a happy
guest, of the beauty of their gardens and the country in which
they dwell, of their good deeds. He writes of miracles wrought
by men whom he once knew, now passing their eternity in
showering joys upon the earth. He writes of things tranquil
and happy and good; only very seldom we hear a note of
trouble, and even this is usually described as of another's burden
rather than his own.

To Leontius, that Bishop of Bordeaux who had brought on
himself the fury of Charibert and a huge fine for affront to
Chlotar's memory, he writes safely and prettily in praise of the
churches Leontius and his wife have raised and adorned, so
many and so beautiful that Leontius is truly "the glory of Bordeaux." Moreover, he merits a weary traveller's gratitude
because he has put wonderful bathrooms into his lovely houses
in the country near by. These stand on the banks of the
Garonne, bordered by meadows that refresh the eye with their
cool grass and bright flowers, near fields of wheat tossing in the
wind, near the stream where one can stand to fish lazily in
heart's content.[40]

Two Bishops of Paris receive greetings. To one, Germanus,
goes a rather sad answer to an invitation: "I am longing to see
you, but the Lady Radegund will not let me come!" The other,
Ragnemod, successor of Germanus in 576, Fortunatus had
known when the prelate was "Rucco" to his friends and a
simple deacon to the Church. It was he, we learn from Gregory,

[40] *H.F.* IV, 26; Ven. Fort. *Carm.* I, 6; 8–13; 15; 19f.

who protected Queen Fredegund in his Cathedral at Paris after the murder of her husband Chilperic. Fortunatus writes to thank him for a present of Parian marble he has given to Radegund and Agnes. Other episcopal rulers in his address-book include Sidonius of Mainz, Nicetius of Trèves, Vilicus of Metz, Egidius of Reims, Martin of Galicia, Avitus of Clermont and Ageric of Verdun. Sidonius has built a baptistery, gift of a daughter of King Theodebert. Of Nicetius Gregory of Tours tells with high praise that he excommunicated Chlotar for his wicked life and received with disdain the penalty of banishment; Sigebert, however, restored him.[41] Fortunatus avoids such an unpleasing topic, and prefers to rhapsodize on the castle of the Bishop of Trèves, built on high rocky cliffs above the river Moselle. From its walls and their thirty towers the guest looks out over fields of grain blowing on the slopes of its hill, over vineyards and orchards, over flower-gardens, over distant boats gliding in the summer time along the river below. So the poet also describes the view from his window in the chateau of Vilicus at Metz, whose hospitality inspired him to concoct during dinner little poems on the exquisite service and food.[42]

An excellent host, too, was Bishop Egidius of Reims, whose food for the body equalled his preaching for the soul! Gregory painted a graver side to the picture, in the condemnation of Egidius for treason to Childebert and his banishment from his See. But both Gregory and Fortunatus agree in praise of Martin of Braga (in Galicia), the Apostle of the Suevi in Spain. He was evidently most learned, and Fortunatus is properly humble before him: "But why," he writes, "my dear Father, do you read into me your own accomplishments and say publicly

[41] *Carm.* II, 9; VIII, 2; III, 26; IX, 10; II, 11; IX, 9. Fortunatus wrote in prose a *Life* of Germanus, and others of Hilary of Poitiers, Albinus of Angers, Paternus of Avranches, Radegund, and Marcellus of Paris; ed. Br. Krusch, *op. cit.* For Ragnemod and Fredegund see *H.F.* VII, 4; for Nicetius, *M.G.H. Epist.* III, pp. 118ff.

[42] *Carm.* III, 12; 13; 13 c, d.

of me what is due to you alone? You understand theology and
are perfectly at home in philosophy. Why, I hardly know even
the names of Plato or Aristotle or Chrysippus or Pittacus!
I haven't read Hilary or Gregory or Ambrose or Augustine, and
if they *should* come to me in a vision, they would find me fast
asleep! And of you yourself I believe that you don't really
delight as much in grand pomp of dogmas as you do in the
doing of good deeds." [43]

One suspects that there was not overmuch research into
Patristic writings in the Chaplain's cheerful study at Holy
Cross!

Lines in verse, composed at the request of Gregory, describe
the converting and baptism of the five hundred Jews at Pentecost by Avitus, Bishop of Clermont in Auvergne. There is also
a letter written with great reverence to this same Bishop on
behalf of Agnes and Radegund. Ageric, the protector of
Guntram-Boso and Bertefried, those turbulent nobles so
bitterly hostile in Austrasia to the rule of Brunhild and her son,
is praised for his skill in theology and for his energy, too, in
building of Churches. Felix of Nantes, the enemy and
accuser of Gregory of Tours, receives verses of the same easy
grace. [44]

More noteworthy than these occasional compositions is the
Easter Hymn addressed to Felix, from which are taken the
two hymns entitled *Salve, festa dies,* still sung by us at Easter
and Ascensiontide. [45]

But Gregory of Tours was chief among the episcopal friends
of Fortunatus. As Gregory had asked, he sent the Bishop his
writings for publication, full, as he laments he is, of fear of

---

[43] III, 15; V, 1 (prose); cf. 2 (verse); *H.F.* X, 19; V, 37.
[44] *Carm.* V, 5; III, 21, 23, 23a; III, 4–8, 10; V, 7. *H.F.* V, 11; IX,
8 and 12; V, 5.
[45] *Carm.* III, 9; *Eng. Hymnal,* Nos. 624 (Maurice Frederick Bell)
and 628 (Percy Dearmer).

their unworthiness: "I have had no one to criticize or improve my work, for I might just as well howl as sing in this country, where people see no difference between the notes of a goose and a swan." He writes to Gregory in terms of affection and respect, tells the people of Tours how fortunate they are to have a Father so holy and so solicitous for them, beloved of Sigebert and of Brunhild their rulers, and composes for him from time to time little informal notes in verse: a birthday greeting; thanks for a gift, a loan, or an invitation; congratulation on a safe return from a journey: "If the note is brief, do not reckon my love by its size." Gregory, on the other hand, seems to have thought more about the skill of Fortunatus in writing than about the writer himself. He relates in his narrative, *Of the virtues of holy Martin,* that he once told his mother about a vision he had had of sick folk healed in Martin's Church. The story was a thrilling one, and, of course, the mother was duly edified at this honour vouchsafed her son. "Why are you so lazy? Why don't you write about these visions of yours?" she complained. Gregory had his answer ready: "You know quite well that I can't write! How could a stupid amateur like me dare to tell of such wonderful deeds of Martin? If only Severus or Paulus were still alive, or at any rate, Fortunatus were here, to describe them! I should only run into trouble if I tried to do it." But Armentaria was shrewder than the Bishop. "Don't you know," she retorted, "that if anyone talks to us in the way you do, in just ordinary language, more people will listen to him? Now make no more ado, but set to work; it will be wicked of you to keep such marvels to yourself." [46]

It is a pleasant little tale, the more so because Gregory hardly mentions Fortunatus in his narrative of the Franks. But he did

[46] *Carm.* Preface, 4ff.; V, 3f., 8ff., 9, 11, 13–17; VIII, 11ff., 14–21; *De virt. S. Mart.* I, Preface.

expect to see his own crude efforts in prose turned by the poet into verse.[47]

There are many poems addressed to persons of eminence in civil life: to Dynamius and to Jovinus, Governors of Provence; to Gogo, tutor of the little King Childebert; to the Duke Bodegisil, Governor of Marseilles; to the Duke Lupus; to Count Berulf. The verses to Gogo show him as one of kindly and generous nature, thinking of charitable deeds with his friend Lupus, Duke of Champagne, whom we have met already as the champion of Brunhild. Berulf is chaffed because Fortunatus is kept waiting at the Count's house for a sorely needed dinner. He was afterward made Duke of Tours and Poitiers by King Sigebert, but fell under suspicion of having stolen the royal treasure, lost his dukedom, and narrowly escaped with his life. A little poem to Gogo shows the same love of good fare: "No, I really can't come to dinner. How could I feast on chicken and goose when I am full of roast beef? In fact, I'm so drowsy that even my verses are falling asleep!" Another somewhat coarse description tells of the effects of a monster feast given the writer by a certain Mummolen, possibly the father of Bodegisil.[48]

A noble list of correspondents, in truth, though scarcely a list of noble subjects. But the letters to royal patrons from this priest are far more astonishing. There is a marriage song for King Sigebert and his bride Brunhild and another poem of rejoicing at her conversion to the Catholic Church. King Charibert, whom we see in Gregory's narrative as excommunicated by Germanus of Paris, as an enemy of the Church and a despiser of clergy, is praised by Fortunatus to the skies. Chil-

[47] Greg. Tur. *In Glor. Conf.* Preface; 44; 94; *H.F.* V, 8; *De virt. S. Mart.* I, 2 and 13. His *In Glor. Martyr.* 41 repeats some of the verses of Fortunatus (from *Carm.* IX, 14).

[48] *Carm.* VI, 9f.; VII, 1–5; 8; 11; 14f.; Greg. Tur. *H.F.* VI, 4; VIII, 26: Dalton, *The History of the Franks*, II, p. 429.

peric, Gregory's "Nero and Herod of our time," receives a
special laudation when a Synod of Bishops meet at the royal
chateau of Berny, near Soissons, to try the poet's friend,
Gregory of Tours himself, on a charge of slandering Queen
Fredegund. The tale of Chilperic's virtues here is long: to his
justice and his skill in battles is added his merit in legislation,
in poetry, in literature, in theology! We may remember Gregory's observations on the last and the destruction worked by
Chilperic on Poitiers itself. The Lady Fredegund stands out
in brilliant light:

> *omnibus excellens meritis Fredegundis opima.*

She had asked the prayers of Radegund for her royal consort.
But not a word is said about Gregory and his suffering.[49]

Two other poems try to comfort Chilperic and Fredegund
in their grief for their little sons Chlodobert and Dagobert.
One was written just after the death of the children, the
other for the Easter following. Here Fortunatus may well
have been touched by the misery of their mother. There is
also an offering to the memory of each of the boys. Chlodobert,
we are told, was fifteen years old, born to magnify the hopes
of the Franks, but now entering upon a better kingdom;
Dagobert died "a baby just shown to earth," taken swiftly
from baptismal waters to his home in light.[50]

Both the elder and the younger Childebert receive special
reverence. The son of Clovis is so distinguished in the mind
of Fortunatus for his devotion to the Church that he writes
these words of the King in a description of the church of
Saint Vincent in Paris which Childebert himself built:

> Melchisedech noster merito rex atque sacerdos
>   conplevit laicus religionis opus.

[49] *Carm.* VI, 1ff.; IX, 1: Greg. Tur. *H.F.* IV, 26, V, 49; *De virt.*
S. Mart. I, 29; Longnon, p. 401. The date of the Synod was 580.
[50] *Carm.* IX, 2–5.

There is another picture of this Childebert as the zealous fre-
quenter of churches in a poem on a garden planted by him
for his wife Ultrogotha. But we hear nothing from Fortunatus
of his many conspiracies for the undoing of his royal brothers,
and not a word of his share with Chlotar in the murder of
his nephews, the boys of Clodomir. The second Childebert
and his mother, the Queen-Regent Brunhild, appear to great
advantage, for Poitiers was in their governance. Fortunatus
journeys with them along the River Moselle from Metz to the
royal castle at Andernach; in their company he enjoys the
beautiful scenery of the vine-clad banks, rising now and again
in steep and rocky cliffs, and brings a keen appetite to the
lunch served on board the boat to the sound of music; at
Andernach the young King watches the salmon fishing from
the castle walls. Touraine had special reason to be grateful to
Childebert the second, because he granted it some immunity
from taxation. Nor does Fortunatus forget this fact.[51]

Most of all this, however, is but part of an endless pouring
out of mediocre verse. Of greater interest is a poem which
pictures the story of the Spanish Princess Galswintha, the little
bride and victim of Chilperic.[52] We see her terrified by evil
foreboding as she leaves the Visigothic Palace at Toledo. The
legates of Chilperic were kept waiting four days while her
father, King Athanagild, hesitated, moved by the grief of his
wife Goisvintha. But since the girl was sought by a mighty
King, who promised as her wedding gift five cities of Aqui-
taine,[53] he thought it well that she should go, and her servants
gathered round to say goodbye with eyes full of tears. All
the Palace seemed to be dreading, it knew not what. Her
mother travelled with her as far as the frontier of Gaul, where
the last farewells were said; then Queen Goisvintha stepped

---

[51] II, 10; VI, 6; X, 7–9, and 11: Greg. Tur. *H.F.* IX, 30.
[52] VI, 5.   [53] Text of Treaty of Andelot: *H.F.* IX, 20.

slowly from the carriage and stood to watch it leave, unable
to move till it had disappeared from sight. Fortunatus himself
saw it passing through Poitiers, all shining with silver, and
Radegund sent a message, for she loved the young Princess.

.Then the tragedy, though in this poem of Fortunatus the
manner of her death is prudently veiled. No name is spoken;
only her nurse finds her dead and bursts into a lament quickly
stopped. Word that her worst fears are realized travels to the
mother in Spain; her only comfort is in the story, repeated
here, of the lamp that fell unquenched and unharmed before
the girl's tomb.

.But it is time to turn to Fortunatus as he works for the
nuns of Holy Cross. From his *Life of Radegund* written in
prose we can see that her austerities grew even stricter here.
Now she lived on vegetables, denying herself fruit or fish or
eggs, and drank only water, with a little honey or the juice of
pears absorbed in it, no wine or native beer. The work of
tending the poor and sick was faithfully continued, sometimes
in supervising the labours of other sisters, but as often as
obedience allowed, in the toil of her own hands. As her particular duty she took all her week's share, and more, of the
routine of household drudgery in the Convent. She carried
away refuse, stoked and stacked the fires, swept the rooms,
drew the water from the well, cleaned the Community's shoes
while the nuns were still asleep, prepared the food, cooked it,
and washed the plates and the kitchen itself when meals were
done. Between duties she returned to her cell to pray, and
she was always first in the chapel for Offices, whether of the
Night or of the Day.

At the beginning of Lent, however, she withdrew even
from the Convent Community into solitary retreat, which
only ended on Easter morning. This disappearing of the Foundress became something of a function among the people of

Poitiers, who climbed on top of buildings around Holy Cross to see the procession which led Radegund to her anchorage of forty days. There she prayed and starved with all vehemence. We have a letter which Caesaria, successor of the more famous first Abbess of that name, the sister of Caesarius, wrote to Radegund about 570 when she forwarded to her from the Convent at Arles a copy of the Caesarian Rule: "I hear that you go too far in your fasting. Please be reasonable in all things. If you weaken your body by over-great abstinence, you will have to indulge in luxuries and untimely relaxations, and then you will not be able to direct your nuns."[54] Her penitential discipline included, however, practices more severe than abstinence from food. Fortunatus tells us that in Lent Radegund wore iron bands around her neck and arms, and iron chains around her body, so tightly drawn that the flesh stood out around and by Eastertide was furrowed in deep grooves. Another favourite penance was to press upon her body a cross of white hot metal and to neglect the hidden sore.

It is not surprising that miracles were laid to the credit of her sanctity while she still lived. Many, we read, were wrought for sufferers who merely called upon her name; Fortunatus affirms that a dead child was recalled to life by the touch of the robe she had worn. On the contrary, the little mouse that ventured near her needlework fell dead at the first impious nibble: *Est et in rebus minimis magna gloria Creatoris*, her chaplain comments.

The nun Baudonivia wrote another *Life* of Radegund shortly after her death.[55] The Convent thought that Fortunatus had been a bit too sparing of details concerning her, in his fear of exaggeration and of too great plenitude of

[54] ed. Gundlach, *M.G.H. Epist. Merov. et Kar. aevi*, I, 452.
[55] See above, note 34.

words; hence the Abbess Dedimia ruled that further description should fill in details of her glory. Baudonivia begins by confessing truly that she has no eloquence and can write only a "countrified" style. We find that whenever she lacks proper words, which happens when she tries to reflect rather than to make statements, she borrows from the writing of Fortunatus, or from the Lives of saints on the shelves of her Convent Library.[56] But she has some interesting memories. Radegund, it seems, was so wrapt in holy joy on Feast-Days that once she absent-mindedly addressed a nun as "Sister Alleluia." She insisted on a persistent round of prayer and sacred study for herself. If ever the nun who read aloud by her bedside while she was resting desisted a moment, supposing her asleep, she would cry instantly: "Why do you stop? Go on with the reading!" She used to finish the whole Night Office before midnight, but was only too happy to recite Matins again with her sisters at the usual hour. She never spoke an ill word, nor allowed others to do so in her presence; she never asked another to do what she had not first done herself. Her prayer was as wide as her thought; she made the nuns join her constantly in intercession for the vexed kingdoms over which her four stepchildren, the sons of Chlotar, were always wrangling. Not in vain had she known the world as Queen.

But Fortunatus has plenty to say of her love of reading. In his description she feasts on the banquet of Holy Rule, on the teachings of Gregory and Basil, of keen Athanasius and gentle Hilary, on the thunder of Ambrose and the lightning of Jerome, on the wellsprings of Augustine, the sweet lines of Sedulius and the shrewd composition of the chronicler Orosius. The extravagant language does not kill literal truth, and we can picture Radegund thirstily seeking instruction from the stream of learned visitors who dined at Holy Cross on Sundays

[56] ed. Krusch, p. 360.

and great Feasts.[57] She must have grown skilled in theology, abstract and ascetic, in sacred poetry and in history both ecclesiastical and secular—a fitting patroness indeed for the Benedictine nuns of the future.

Sometimes, as we have seen, Radegund and the Lady Abbess Agnes softened a little the rigour of convent life. To their Chaplain Agnes is "Sister" and Radegund is "Mother," a private interchange of the titles they would naturally bear. Often little notes, thrown off in verse, travel from the Priest's house to one or the other nun; sometimes informal gifts go with the notes. He rejoices in elegiacs that Agnes and Radegund have adorned the altar with spring flowers which bring happy strife of colour into a place of peace. He sends a bunch to remind Radegund of their home in Paradise; may she draw him thither by her merits! Another handful of flowers bears a friendly greeting: "Lilies I have not; roses need money. So here are just some violets from my own garden. Yet their colour is royal purple, and even common flowers are really roses, if they are sent in love." So he assures her in her long Lenten retreat that his "thought passes through its doors and will welcome her back." Many gifts are marked for both Radegund and Agnes: chestnuts gathered from the fields or fruit found growing wild in the woods.[58]

So, too, we have poem after poem written to thank the Sisters for presents of delights for his own table: flowers, milk, eggs and fruit and chicken: "White eggs and black grapes! I hope there won't be war in my stomach. You bade me have two eggs for my supper. I had four, really. May I always obey you as my gluttony did today!"; "Thank you so much, my Sister Agnes, for that blanc-mange engraved with its pattern by our own hand"; "I am just stuffed with the

[57] *Carm.* VIII, 1, ll. 53ff.; *Vita Rad.* 18.
[58] *Carm.* VIII, 6–9; XI, 13 and 18: Greg. Tur. *H.F.* IX, 42.

lovely things you sent before! Now here are fresh joys of
butter and milk, and I shall get fatter than ever." Twice
Fortunatus has to decline luxuries on plea of his doctor's
orders; once he begs his friends to pray that he sin not griev-
ously through indulgence of appetite."[59]

The writer had done well to stop here, before his honest
affection for these holy women led him to words better left
unsaid. One cannot blame him very harshly for his dreadful
four hundred lines of verse *On Virginity,* addressed to the
Lady Agnes. This was according to the manner of the day,
and did but follow in the path of Jerome's exhortation to the
girl Eustochium, or of the long poem of the Bishop Avitus to
his sister on the same subject. It is when he wails because he
cannot see Radegund in her retreat, or Agnes in her cloister,
that he shows more sincerity than wisdom. "The light of
mine eyes has disappeared," he writes to Radegund; "the days
are sunless; nothing I see matters now. May these hours of
Lent hurry swiftly on their way!"; "Best of mothers, we beg
you, Agnes and I, relieve the anxiety of us, your two children,
by drinking a little wine. 'Tis but what Paul imposed on
Timothy"; "This month of Lent, Radegund, short as its days
are, seems longer than a whole year. Easter light will seem
doubly radiant when you come to see us from your cell."
When Radegund has at length reappeared, he sends her a
cry of joy: "Now Easter must have *two* celebrations! Surely
it is harvest instead of sowing-time, for no land can seem
bare now you are back." So, too, Agnes is "the delight of
his soul." Absence from her is fasting, and food has no
power to satisfy save she be near; her words are the best of
feasts. It is not surprising that another poem assures his "honoured Mother and dear Sister," the Abbess Agnes, that he loves

[59] *Carm.* XI, 20; 14; 22; 16; 19; 12; 9. For translations from Fortunatus see Helen Waddell, *Mediaeval Lyrics,*[4] pp. 58ff.; Jack Lindsay,
op. cit., pp. 3off.

her with the pure affection of spirit alone, even as if she were his own sister Titiana. He cannot say too much, lest his affections be misconstrued by the horrid words of whispering tongues.[60]

It was not for this innocent gaiety that Fortunatus was canonized by the Church! The Convent chaplain had sterner tasks to perform for his nuns. He begs their prayers when he starts out on dangerous journeys on their behalf: on land through ice and snow, on water in a frail boat tossed by storm. He writes for Radegund under her name the story of the destruction of her native Thuringia, and tells of her longing to see once again its Prince, her cousin Amalafrid, who had served as officer of Justinian's army at Constantinople.[61]

Among these labours for the Convent is found the real reason why Fortunatus is honoured by the Church and remembered, in awareness or in ignorance, by the faithful of these days, who still sing each spring and each May and September from his hymns on the True Cross. Their writing was due to the eagerness of Radegund that her Convent should be hallowed by the presence of sacred relics. According to her disciple Baudonivia she had already begged from Jerusalem a portion of the body of Saint Mammes the martyr; and his little finger had been received by her and her Sisters after a whole week of preparation in prayer and fasting. Other prizes were gathered in, also, for her joy. But her ambition longed to follow the steps of Saint Helena. So she wrote to King Sigebert, as Lord of the territory, begging his permission to seek a fragment of the True Cross from the treasure held by the Emperor in Constantinople. He allowed her prayer, and a mission was despatched to seek this great boon from

[60] *Carm.* VIII, 3; XI, 2 and 4; VIII, 9f.; XI, 16 and 6.
[61] XI, 25f.; *App.* 1 and 3.

Justin and the Empress Sophia. It was granted, and the pilgrims set out on their return journey, bearing their treasures in a magnificent reliquary, of which part is still guarded in the convent of Sainte-Croix at Poitiers, a casing of gold adorned with early Byzantine enamelling and precious stones. Two richly ornamented copies of the Gospels were also sent as a mark of friendship from the Eastern Court.[62]

On their arrival, however, a difficulty arose. Only a bishop could receive this treasure with fitting ceremonial, and, obviously, the Bishop of Poitiers was the prelate to officiate. But the Bishop of this time, Maroveus, as Gregory of Tours tells us, would do nothing of the kind. He even called for his horses when he received Radegund's petition, and withdrew to his house in the country. In her distress she again sent word to King Sigebert. Would he please ask one of the Austrasian bishops to pontificate in the ceremony? Eufronius, Bishop of Tours, was chosen, and under his blessing the gift was borne to its safe keeping in the Convent, with chant of psalms, with procession of clergy and of acolytes, with lighted candles and clouding censers.[63]

The hymns sung on this occasion were the *Pange, lingua, gloriosi proelium certaminis,* and the *Vexilla regis prodeunt.*[64] A third hymn by Fortunatus on the Holy Cross, the *Crux benedicta nitet,* is not so well known. It may have been sung on the same occasion as the two discussed above, or it was perhaps suggested to him by a Cross around which a vine was growing in the Convent garden. It has been translated

[62] Baudonivia, *Vita Radeg.* 14; 16: Greg. Tur. *H.F.* IX, 40: Conway, *The Antiquaries Journal,* III, 1923, pp. 1ff.
[63] Baudonivia, *Vita Radeg.* 16: Greg. Tur. *ibid.* For visits of pilgrims seeking healing from this relic, see *H.F.* VI, 29.
[64] *Carm.* II, 2; 6. On these hymns and their translations see Julian, *Dictionary of Hymnology*[2]; A. S. Walpole, *Early Latin Hymns,* pp. 164ff. The word "Hymn" in the title of the *Vexilla regis* points to singing and music. Two other compositions (*Carm.* II, 4f.) are written in the form of a Cross, according to the bizarre fashion of the time.

by Dr. Neale in the metre of its original, the elegiac couplet.
The last two lines show interwoven thought of the Cross and
the altars of the Church:

> Appensa est vitis inter tua brachia, de qua
>   dulcia sanguineo vina rubore fluunt:
> Fast in thy arms is enfolded the Vine; from whom in
>   its fulness,
> Floweth the blood-red juice, wine that gives life
>   to the soul.[65]

The writing of all is renowned for its form: especially in
the rhymes of the *Vexilla regis,* "the first rhyming hymn in
the Latin language," and the sonorous roll of the trochaic
tetrameters in the *Pange, lingua,* here "first grouped into
stanzas." Part of the former runs:

> Arbor decora et fulgida,
>   ornata regis purpura,
>   electa digno stipite
>   tam sancta membra tangere!
>
> Beata cuius brachiis
>   pretium pependit saeculi!
>   statera facta est corporis
>   praedam tulitque Tartari.

More lovely is the processional music in trochaic rhythm
of the *Pange, lingua:*

> Crux fidelis, inter omnes arbor una nobilis
> (nulla talem silva profert flore fronde germine)
> dulce lignum, dulce clavo, dulce pondus sustinens!
>
> Flecte ramos, arbor alta, tensa laxa viscera,
> et rigor lentescat ille quem dedit nativitas,
> ut superni membra regis mite tendas stipite.

---

[65] *Carm.* II, 1; Nisard, trans. *Venance Fortunat,* 1887, p. 76, note 1.
The two lines in English are taken from the translations by Dr. Neale:
Encyclopaedia Metropolitana,[2] *Rom. Lit.,* pp. 236ff. On the Cross inter-
twined with the vine in mediaeval art see Grisar, *Hist. of Rome and the
Popes in the Middle Ages,* III, pp. 195ff.

The translation of Dr. Neale is known to all. No one who
has heard these lines fittingly sung in their English rendering,
far more in their Latin original, can doubt for a moment the
depth of spiritual character that lay hidden behind the gay
verses of this poet, courtier and guest of this world. His
hymns on the Cross belong to the time when art, also, was
developing expression of the Crucified as conqueror of sin in
His redemption of mankind: clad in the *tunica clavata*, with
the sun and moon above His head in token of supreme sover-
eignty.[66] They have been sung through the centuries whenever the Cross has gone forth to conquer, at home or in the
mission field. Few worshippers in modern days, however,
hark back in mind to the day when they first accompanied
the solemn Procession of the Cross in Poitiers.

In 587 Radegund's life drew to its end; Gregory of Tours
and the nun Baudonivia have left us a picture of her passing
on the thirteenth of August. Maroveus, her Bishop, was
absent from Poitiers, engaged in Visitations at different parts
of his diocese, and Gregory of Tours recited the prayers for
the dead, leaving to Maroveus the solemn celebration of the
Requiem Mass and the covering of the coffin in its tomb.
Miracles attended the funeral procession of the Saint and her
burial in the Church of Saint Mary, which she herself had
founded outside the walls of Poitiers.[67]

The present church and its famous tomb are sought by
thousands of pilgrims every year from all parts of France,
especially during the Novena of Saint Radegund in August.
The church bears her name and is approached by the Rue
Sainte-Croix and the Rue Sainte-Radegonde. Near it runs

[66] See G. Schönermark, *Der Crucifixus in der bildenden Kunst,* 1908,
pp. 28ff., and note the same characteristics in the representation of the
Crucified Lord sent to Queen Theodelinda by Gregory the Great (pp. 30f.);
cf. Otto Zöckler, *The Cross of Christ,* pp. 192ff.

[67] Greg. Tur. *In Glor. Conf.* 104; *H.F.* IX, 2: Baudonivia, *Vita Radeg.*
21ff.

the river, and it can be well seen from the Pont-Neuf, which bridges the waters here. Its walls are covered with tablets of thanksgiving for her intercession, and its windows tell the story of her life. In a little recess on the south side, the Chapelle du Pas de Dieu, is a figure of Radegund clothed in her royal mantle with crown and rosary, kneeling before a figure of our Lord, reverenced after a somewhat literal manner. For the mark of His footstep, printed in the floor between the figures, is continually venerated by the prayers and offerings of the faithful.[68] The tomb lies underneath the church in a crypt. It was wrought of black marble in the eighth or the ninth century but now holds only a few relics of the Saint, since marauding bands of Protestants pillaged the shrine in 1562 and burned her body. Other relics, saved from the fire, were sent to the keeping of the Convent of Holy Cross.[69] Candles break the darkness and reveal a crowned statue of Radegund, given in 1658 by Anne of Austria in thanksgiving for the healing of Louis XIV. Not only in Poitou, but in many other places where men pray: in Churches of the Somme, of the Vienne, of the Aisne, and of the Loire; in Italy and Belgium and Austria, altars and statues still revere Saint Radegund. In England her memory is honoured in various dedications: of the renowned convent of Saint Mary and Saint Radegund in Cambridge, dating from the twelfth century till the fifteenth, when its buildings were given to the foundation of Jesus College; of Saint Radegund's Abbey, now in ruins, a Premonstratensian foundation of the twelfth century at Bradsole, near Dover; of the churches at Grayingham in Lincolnshire, at Sinton in Yorkshire, of Postling in Kent, of Whitwell in the Isle of Wight. In Canterbury a street still bears her name.[70]

[68] *ibid.* 20. The Feast of this Apparition is observed in Poitiers on August 3.
[69] E. Briand, *Sainte Radegonde,* pp. 323f.   [70] *ibid.* pp. 409ff.

The Lady Abbess Agnes died in the same year, and with the passing of his friends Fortunatus felt that his work at Holy Cross was done. Somewhere about 598 he succeeded Plato, whose consecration he had marked earlier in a little poem, as Bishop of Poitiers.[71] For us at least his writings have now come to an end. We may think of him, if we will, at the end of the line of ancient Latin poets: in his classical metres, in his borrowings from their verses, especially in his love of Vergil. We place him better as facing the future, first of the line of Latin mediaeval poets, turning his skill away from quantity toward accent and rhyme in the noblest of his verses: telling of feasting and of love, of nature's beauty in the springtide, of friendship and its delight, of men and their doings and their deeds, of sorrow at the passing of the dead, of the Church and of her Lord. His prose is simple when it tells of Saints, tortuous when it is used for his letters in the Latin of the time, with manifold forms and words and turns of phrase that classical Latin never knew.[72] Yet for him, as for his fellows, this Latin finds a compensation in a freshness of joy in living, physical and spiritual, that is stimulating in its picture of humanity, a reawakening to new life that the dying age of the Empire could not know.[73]

[71] *Carm.* X, 14.
[72] See, for detailed study, Tardi, pp. 211ff.
[73] H. O. Taylor, *Class. Heritage of the Middle Ages,*[3] pp. 294ff.

CHAPTER III

A PICTURE OF BRITAIN

"There are no authentic chronicles of the Saxon Conquest. The Britons in their refuge among the Welsh mountains relapsed into Celtic barbarism, and if the priest Gildas wrote for them a Book of Lamentations in Latin, it answers few of the purposes of history."

No remark could be truer than this, by a modern historian.[1] Yet, as another has remarked, the writing of Gildas "is the only work at all which throws any light on public affairs in Britain in the sixth century."[2] And when we have done with Gildas the "historian," we have, further, some thought of interest in Gildas the priest, and, more especially, in Gildas the monk of these early British times.

He was not really an historian at all. He wrote because he could keep silence no longer, when, as the Psalmist before him, he had kept his mouth with a bridle while the wickedness of his country lay in his vision for ten weary years. To utter his thought was a task, he declared, that needed courage, and he struggled a long time, held "as it were in the narrow vestibule of fear." But by his own reasonings and the prayers of his brethren he was at last constrained to inveigh passionately against the "inky blackness" of "the unspeakable and monstrous sins of his age."

[1] G. M. Trevelyan, *History of England*, 1926, p. 33.
[2] Mommsen, ed. Gildas, *Chron. Min.* III, p. 9. Cf. F. Lot, *Medieval Studies*, pp. 262ff.: R. H. Hodgkin, *History of the Anglo-Saxons*, 1935, pp. 60; 76ff.; 118ff. Gildas has also been edited, with translation, by H. Williams, *Cymmrodorion Record Series*, III, 1899. Cf. for the *De Excidio, PL* LXIX.

It is a preacher, then, that we have here;[3] as Salvian in the fifth century saw the vengeance of God descending on the Romans in punishment for the sins of the Empire, so Gildas declares that British greed and violence are paying their merited penalty. Repentance is the only hope. True enough. But it is rather hard for us that in our lack of knowledge it is this storm of reproaches, with its vague references here and there to facts, which must be keenly probed and discussed. It springs from the early twilight of British days; where Arthur flits from deed to deed of bold and chivalrous romance; where Celtic kings war one on another from their lairs in the hills of Wales or on the moors of Devon and Cornwall, far from the grasp of the encroaching Saxons; where in valley or isle or on some river-bank the primitive British hermits are building their rude oratories, destined to become Britain's first schools of sacred and secular learning under austere rule of study and penitence.

The modern reader must not lack courage if he will attack this uncouth jeremiad. Gildas himself had no illusions about his literary merits, though he had read his Vergil and, probably, Juvenal and Claudian, as well as some Christian writers. Its name has come down to us in varying forms,[4] which we may summarize as "The Complaint of Gildas the Wise on the ruin and miseries of Britain." The diffidence of its author caused him repeatedly to refer to his "little work," which elsewhere he terms a "letter," addressed openly to the Church and State of Britain at large.[5] At one point he described it as his "so tearful and plaintive history," [6] though the word "historia" means here simply his description of the troubles of his land. In the dearth of authorities for his time, later writers

---

[3] Ebert, *Gesch. d. Lit. d. Mittelalters*, I,[2] pp. 564f.
[4] Mommsen, ed. pp. 10f.
[5] "opusculum," cc. 62; 94; "epistula," cc. 1; 93.
[6] c. 37.

did look upon him as a serious historian. To Bede he was the "historian of the British," one of the chief sources available for early British history; and writers of the Middle Ages gave him the proud title of "historiographus."

Throughout this "letter" he writes as a British citizen of the Roman empire to his countrymen under allegiance to the same power.[7] The British, in his eyes, are a faithless people, incapable of loyal service, professing obedience to their Roman conquerors and benefactors, but quick to rebel, once given the chance. Thus, directly the Roman army had been withdrawn, "the treacherous British lioness" slaughtered the officials whom Rome had left behind to rule her in full confidence of peace, and caused the hasty return of another Roman army to crush these "cunning foxes" of Celtic Britain.[8] Their courage, however, was no greater than their loyalty, and they offered no resistance to those who came to crush their rebellion.

It is their luxury-loving spirit that is to blame. They dwell in a land of wide plains and pleasant hills, watered especially by two great rivers, the Thames and the Severn, along which sail the boats bringing delicacies for British comfort from foreign ports. Once there were twenty-eight cities, and fortresses with embattled towers on their gates, and sturdy walls, looking out on meadows bright with flowers and streams gliding drowsily past in quiet peace. That was when Britain was willingly controlled by Rome. When the British rose up against their rulers, the Roman sword was unsheathed to strike sharply for deeper conquest. British coins now were to

[7] The Latin language is "nostra lingua": c. 23; Mommsen, ed. p. 9.

[8] It is not necessary to deal here with all the surmises that have been made on historical questions in Gildas. "The lioness" may be Boudicca (Zimmer, *Nennius Vindicatus*, p. 105), or may refer in general to Britain (Williams, ed. p. 20). On the thorns that bristle around Gildas as "historian" see the editions of Mommsen and of Williams; also C. Gross, *Sources and Literature of English History*,[2] pp. 245f., and other authorities mentioned in my note 2.

give place to Roman coins marked with the Emperor's head, and "Britannia" henceforth must yield to "Romania," in fact, if not in name. So runs our "history" here.

As time went on, Rome found it difficult in the midst of her own troubles to keep guard and control over this distant part of her dominion. Moreover, the British were continually at strife with one another as well as with their rulers. Gildas tells us that "thickets of tyrants sprang up within the island and spread out into a vast forest, so that Britain held neither Roman customs nor laws." He relates also that she herself sent forth for the Empire a tyrant, Maximus, "a shoot of her own most bitter growth," and that the departure of Maximus weakened the island terribly by depriving it of great numbers of her young warriors, who marched out in 383 and never came back again.

We cannot tell now how far this is true. But already in the fourth century invaders from various directions were harassing the coasts of Britain: the Picts from Scotland, reinforced by the Scots who came across the sea from their home in Ireland, and the Saxons sailing over the water from Germany. We read here of three great inroads of Picts and Scots. Thrice the British sent appeals to Rome for aid, "huddling like frightened chickens beneath the comforting wings of their parents." Twice Roman soldiers came to drive away the enemy: "flying on horseback like eagles to slaughter the fierce aggressors till they fell thick and fast, as leaves fall in their due season; storming as a mountain torrent on their path of retribution." Even the wrath of Gildas at his countrymen cannot make him forget his love of pictures, and similes and metaphors abound in his "complaint." For their defence the British built under Roman orders a wall of turf to keep out the northern invaders, and when that proved inadequate were forced to spend their monies public and private in raising a stronger barrier from sea to sea. The story here is full of errors.[9]

And to no avail, it goes on. The Picts and Scots, when the Romans had departed, sailed again across the "vale of Tithys," disembarking from their rough boats "like worms creeping from their holes in the warmth of the sun." They seized British lands in the north and advanced as far as the defending line, where Gildas describes the British as too cowardly for battle, too frightened to run, sitting still till they were knocked off their wall, a pathetic prey. To this distress from without was added the peril of robbery from within, as the starving natives attacked each other to gain the food of which the pirates had despoiled them.

Again approach was made to Rome, and Gildas gives here a record of real interest, and very possibly true, in a letter addressed: "To Agitius, consul for the third time, the laments of the Britons." It is a sad tale: "the barbarians drive us to the sea, the sea drives us to the barbarians, and so we have a choice of miseries and are either murdered or drowned." No other contemporary record supports this message, written, of course, to Aetius, minister and general of Valentinian the third and of Galla Placidia, who held his third consulship in 446.[10]

But by now the Roman Empire in the West was herself in the grip of her last struggle with her own enemies. Not all at once, but slowly, little by little, the officials whom she had once sent year after year to aid the Britons—the Count of Britain, the Duke of the Britains, the Count of the Saxon Shore in Britain—were ceasing to come at so great an expense to Roman citizens. Doubtless, Rome neither expected nor

[9] For criticism see F. Haverfield, *The Romanization of Roman Britain*, 1923, p. 87; R. G. Collingwood, *Roman Britain*, 1936, pp. 293f., 298ff.
[10] Bede gives it in the part of his *Ecclesiastical History* that draws upon Gildas; I, cc. 12ff.

intended permanent severance of Britain from her Empire;
even if shortly after 408, when the Saxons had come down
on Britain in their multitude, the Emperor Honorius had
ruled that "the Britons must themselves see to the defending
of their own island." [11]

When Aetius was consul in 446, the Saxons had already
been settling on the British coasts for some twenty years and
could no longer be dislodged.[12] For a short while the Picts
and Scots were kept at bay by a people driven through famine
to descend on their enemies from secret retreats in mountain
caves and depths of the forest. But plague worked havoc upon
these natives of Britain, and their own wild chieftains
swooped down from high strongholds upon their fields and
cattle and men; till at last in their need they had recourse to
the desperate expedient of inviting the Saxons, "hateful to
God and men," to aid them against the Picts and Scots. Then
"the crowd of whelps from the den of the barbarous she-wolf"
came in three long ships of war to fix their claws in the East
of Britain, to demand yearly tribute of provisions, to deal
ruin far and wide.

This, then, is the picture given by Gildas of the state of his
country after the Saxon advances:—

"The fire heaped up by the sacrilegious hands of these
invaders of our Eastern shore rose high in just vengeance on
our crimes from sea to sea. It ravaged the cities and districts
that lay near and did not abate till it had consumed in ashes
nearly all the surface of our island and licked the western
ocean with its fierce red tongue. So for us in actual fact is
fulfilled that which the prophet said with mourning of the
Assyrian assault upon Judaea: They have burned Thy
sanctuary with fire to the ground; they have polluted the

[11] Zosimus, VI, 10.
[12] Bury, *L.R.E.* I, p. 201; cf. R. H. Hodgkin, *Hist. Anglo-Saxons,* p. 68.

tabernacle of Thy Name. And again: God, the heathen have
come into Thine inheritance; they have defiled Thy holy
Temple. And thus it was that by many blows of the batter-
ing-ram all towns and all their inhabitants, with the rulers
of the Church, with priests and people, were laid low upon
the ground among flashing swords and crackling flames. It
was a pitiful sight to look upon, in the places where streets
behold the foundation-stones of towers and lofty walls over-
thrown from their hinges: the holy altars, the fragments of
dead bodies covered with blood congealed and stiff, all
mingled as if in some terrible wine-press. No place of burial
was there anywhere except the ruins of houses and the bellies
of beasts and birds; no reverence save for the souls of holy
men, if indeed there *were* many holy souls found whom the
angels might bear to high heaven at this time. For the good
vine had degenerated then into bitterness; so that rarely, as
the prophet told, was seen a bunch of grapes or an ear of
corn, so to speak, behind the backs of those who gathered or
reaped. And, therefore, among the wretched survivors some
were caught in the mountains and slaughtered in heaps;
others, exhausted by hunger, yielded themselves to the enemy
for life-long slavery, if they were not granted immediate
death, their highest boon. Others sought lands across the sea
with loud wails, chanting this boat-song in rhythm with
their oars beneath the swelling sails: 'Thou hast given us as
sheep for the banquet, and among the heathen Thou hast
scattered us.' Others on the mountain crags, threatening and
precipitous, in deep ravines and on the cliffs of the sea-coast,
dragged on their lives, ever full of suspicion and fear, yet
still in their native land." [13]

There is good reason to believe, as we shall see later, that

---

[13] cc. 24f. The flight across the sea refers to migrations of Celts during
this century from Britain to Brittany (Armorica).

Gildas lived in the West of Britain. His narrative is therefore of interest here for its apparent theory that destruction from the hands of the Saxons landing on the Eastern coast "advanced rapidly across the centre of the island till it touched the Western sea at some point, and that the invaders then withdrew to some extent from the West, leaving blank ruin behind." [14] This would imply that they crossed the country in one great marauding force, rather than that they ravaged Britain separately by small bands acting in different districts. Their ravaging, Gildas tells, was followed by a withdrawal of Saxon invaders, and subsequently by a triumph for the British under a Roman general of high birth, Ambrosius Aurelianus, "whose son now in these days of ours has degenerated from the noble character of his fathers." It looks from this as though Ambrosius had fought and conquered some considerable time before Gildas was writing.[15] Then came a period in which British and Saxons alternated in victory and defeat, till finally a great battle took place at Badon Hill, summed up by Gildas as "almost the last slaughter wrought by us on that scum of the earth." He continues: "But the cities of my native land were no longer dwelt in as before; up to this day they lie deserted in neglect and ruins. For even though foreign wars have ceased, civil strife has not come to an end."

It seems, then, that the battle of Badon Hill brought to an end for a time the Saxon inroads into, at least, the West of Britain. Its exact place and date are uncertain; but if Mommsen is correct in dating it about 500, the ravages of seventy years of Saxon occupation were still a melancholy

[14] See Trevelyan, pp. 37ff.; cf. R. H. Hodgkin, pp. 118ff., and R. G. Collingwood, p. 318, who infers, from the evidence of archaeology, ruin by evacuation, not by fire and sword.
[15] Mommsen, p. 9. See, however, Oman, *England before the Norman Conquest,*[6] p. 201.

sight in the middle of the sixth century when Gildas was writing. Badon Hill itself is usually considered as belonging to Bath in Somerset.[16] Myth has invested it with some of the romance of Arthur, thought of in his legend from time to time as the hero who rallied the British to victory here. But Gildas says nothing of Arthur in any part of his writings.[17]

There is a kernel of truth, we may think, then, in this tale of the past, wrapped about by the fibre of worthless detail. But now, when Gildas attacks his own day, he becomes much more reliable, and we may read with more attention as he sharpens his pen for the castigating of individuals: to wit, the Five Kings of Britain.[18] With the coming of peace to the West of Britain, he now declares, all thought of self-control and of moderation, of truth and of justice has vanished. These are no Kings, but tyrants, robbers, perjurers, adulterers: given to lies and hypocrisy; favouring the wicked, despising the humble; pretending to revere the altars of the Church but in reality scorning them.

First, there is Constantine, "the tyrannical whelp of the foul lioness of Dumnonia." His special offences are: first, that he has cast away his lawful wife for another woman; secondly, that in the disguise of a reverend Abbot he has murdered at the very altar itself two boys, torn from the keep-

[16] Badbury in Dorset was held to be the site by Guest, followed by Freeman and by Green. Against Guest see W. H. Stevenson, *English Hist. Review*, XVII, p. 633; for Bath, Williams ed. p. 62. Bede gives the date as c. 493 (ed. Plummer, II, pp. 30f.); the *Annales Cambriae* (*M.H.B.* I. ed. Petrie and Sharpe, 1848, p. 830), as 516. For the date c. 500 see Mommsen ed. p. 9; cf. Zimmer, *Nenn. Vind.* p. 100. For other theories see Oman, pp. 200f.

[17] J. Rhys: *Celtic Britain,*[3] pp. 108; 236ff.; *Annales Cambriae, M.H.B.* I, *ibid.*: Nennius, *Hist. Britt.* c. 56.

[18] The work was wrongly divided here by Gale in his edition of 1691 into *Historia Gildae* (cc. 1-26) and *Epistola Gildae* (cc. 27-110). One of the two MSS. still existing (Ff I. 27, Cambridge Library) still shows this division, the other (Dd I. 17, *ibid.*) shows only one work, as seems to have been the case in the lost Cottonian MS. used by the first editors of Gildas, Polydore Vergil (1525) and Josselin (1568). There is no internal evidence for the division, and modern editors do not make it.

ing of both their natural mother and their spiritual mother, Holy Church, together with the tutors who had them in charge. Later story had it that these two boys were the sons of Modad, Arthur's nephew; that they had joined the Saxons to fight against Constantine and in defeat had sought sanctuary; that Constantine had pursued them to their sacred refuge and had put them to death.[19]

Dumnonia corresponded to the modern Devon and Cornwall, and an attempt has been made to show that this wicked King Constantine was converted by Saint Petroc and became Constantine the hermit, so greatly revered in Cornwall, whose memory still hovers about the ruin of Saint Constantine's Church and around Constantine Bay near Padstow.[20] But the evidence does not support this connection. Constantine was a very common name in Romanized Britain among those who honoured the first Christian Emperor of Rome; and the Constantine held in the pious memory of Cornish Churches is doubtless some other hero of Dumnonia, who lived at a later date when it was considerably less in area.[21]

The second King among these five sinners was Aurelius Caninus, whom Gildas calls the "lion's whelp." His kingdom is not named, though probably it included the country north and south of the Severn: Somerset, Gloucestershire and part of South Wales, with his capital perhaps, at Caerleon, "the City of the Legions." [22] He had been guilty of stirring up civil wars for his own profiting. Let him beware, mindful of the untimely deaths of his kin; for now he is left alone as a dried-up tree in the midst of a plain. The third, Vortipor,

[19] Geoffrey of Monmouth, XI, 3f.
[20] S. Baring-Gould and John Fisher, *Lives of the British Saints*, II, s.v. *Constantine, King, Confessor*, pp. 170ff.
[21] See Canon G. H. Doble, *St. Constantine, King and Monk, and St. Merryn, "Cornish Saints" Series*, No. 26. For the Cornish Saint Constantine converted by Petroc see the *Life of Petroc, Nova Legenda Anglie*, ed. Carl Horstman, II, 1901, p. 319.
[22] Zimmer, *Nenn. Vind.* p. 307.

was King of Demetia, which corresponded roughly to Pembrokeshire. To Gildas he is like a leopard in his multicoloured habits and vices, and his reign is filled with a full record of crime and lust, since his hair is now gray. The fourth bore the name of Cuneglas, which Gildas says means "tawny butcher" in Latin.[23] We are not told where he lived, but we may imagine him as Lord over part of Wales. He seems to have been of the clan of the Bear, and he, too, was stained with crime.[24] He had cast away his wife to look after another woman, her wicked sister, already vowed in her widowhood to a life of chastity. His evil deeds call forth constantly groans and sighs from the saints whom he has injured, though like a savage lioness some day they shall crunch his bones in vengeance. Let him repent betimes, or he will burn in a fearful globe of everlasting fire without relief of death.

But of all these Kings the most romantic in imagination is the fifth, Maelgwn of Gwynedd (in Latin *Venedotia*), Lord of Northern Wales and "Dragon of the Island," as he is called here, whether "the island" refers to his dominion in Anglesey or to the land of Britain itself. God had made him higher in power than almost all the other Kings of Britain, and, like the dragon in the Apocalypse, he ruled the union of leopard and lion and bear. Yet, if his power was greater, his character was worse. In his early youth with his companions, bold as lions, he had cut down with sword and fire a King, his own uncle, whom some have imagined as Arthur, though Gildas is silent on this detail.[25] His was a name full of dread throughout the mountain regions of Snowdonia, a shadow brooding over its wild passes and precipices, terrible alike to the Celts in their lonely farms and huts and to the

---

[23] butcher-dog (cune, canis) ? See F. Lot, *Med. Studies*, p. 252.

[24] *ibid.* For a suggestion that Cuneglas had once been the charioteer of Arthur (=the bear-man), see Oman, pp. 211f. Collingwood discusses the possibility that he was Arthur himself (pp. 320f.).

[25] John Rhys, *Studies in the Arthurian Legend*, p. 8. On Maelgwn see J. E. Lloyd, *History of Wales*, I, pp. 128ff.

freebooters who might seek to penetrate through their clouds and mist in search of plunder.

He had not always been so. Gildas relates that he had once upon a time repented of his sin and dedicated himself to the monastic life, fleeing to refuge as a dove from the hawk. Mother Church had rejoiced to see that day. But the devil caught him back to hell, and now he hears no longer the songs of Sion among the shouts of his own lying band of revellers. There is still a hint of something big in this royal chieftain, "more lavish than his kind in evil, more generous in giving; mightier in arms, bolder for the destruction of his own soul." After his return to his savage ways, monk though he was, he had taken to himself a wife, and this, too, not the one whom he had left for the house of the Lord, but another woman, wife of a living man and that his own nephew. Further, he had crowned his misdeeds by the murder of both the woman he had forsaken and the nephew he had robbed. Among the maze of reproaches that Gildas weaves here we can perhaps catch sight of Maelgwn torn between sinful passion of the flesh, strong as his own strong nature, and some remembrance of the words of the monk to whom he once had turned when he was "gnawed night and day by the consciousness of his sins." He could not be ignorant of his deadly offences, for it was his reproach that he had enjoyed as teacher "the cultured master of almost all Britain." No name is given, but we may think that Gildas speaks here of his own Abbot, the great Saint Illtyd.[26]

How Maelgwn made himself supreme over other kings of Britain we do not know. It has been suggested that his ancestor Cunedda had gained and handed down as heirloom the power formerly exercised by the Roman officer called "Duke of the Britains."[27] But here, as elsewhere, the spider

[26] Saint Cadoc has also been suggested: Rhys, *Celtic Britain*, p. 122.
[27] *ibid.* p. 121. A similar suggestion has ascribed to Arthur the power formerly held by the Roman *Comes Britanniae*: Rhys, *Studies*, p. 7.

of legend has been busy about his memory. We are told that when the Welsh chieftains of the sixth century met in contest by the seashore to decide which of them should preside over the others, one of the supporters of Maelgwn placed him in a winged chair. The struggle for power lasted long, and suddenly all were caught by the incoming tide and hastily retreated; all except Maelgwn, whose chair bore him up triumphantly to lordship over all. The place was afterwards called "Maelgwn's Strand." [28] The story seems to show, at any rate, that Maelgwn by his cunning won supremacy over his fellows.

More formidable is the tradition of his death, said to have been due to a scourge of yellow fever about the year 547. [29] A mile and a half from Llandudno there remains still the Eglwys Rhôs, the little church of Llan Rhôs, near the Bryn or Mount of Maelgwn. To this church Maelgwn fled in terror of the prophecy by which the bard Taliesin had declared his coming doom:

> From the Marsh of Rhianedd
> A monster shall come
> On Maelgwn of Gwynedd
> For ill to strike home.
> All golden her ringlets,
> Her tooth and her eye,
> And by her King Maelgwn
> Of Gwynedd shall die!

This fearsome fiend was the Yellow Death personified. She came to the church and stared through the window at the King, who promptly fell sick of her fever and died. [30]

---

[28] Rhys, *Celtic Britain*, p. 125.

[29] *Annales Cambriae*, p. 831; Life of St. Teilo, *Liber Landavensis*, ed. W. J. Rees, p. 101; Lloyd, I, p. 131.

[30] *ibid.* p. 68. For this translation and the original Welsh see *Y Cymmrodor* V, 1882, p. 167. For traditions of Maelgwn in the lives of the saints, confirming him as *largior in dando,* and for the story of his death, see Lloyd, *op. cit.* pp. 129ff.

And now Gildas proceeds to support these rebukes by a flood of quotations from the Bible: Old Testament and New, and the apocryphal writings. A word is, therefore, in place here with regard to the Biblical texts on which he drew. His source, it seems, was most commonly the Vulgate of St. Jerome, though considerable use was made of an old Latin text.[81] Readings are also found in his quotations which correspond exactly neither with the Vulgate nor with the old Latin texts as found elsewhere. These may belong, at least in part, to a separate Irish (or British) recension, based on an old Latin text of the African family. In some cases the Latin text of Gildas corresponds with that of the Codex Vaticanus of the Septuagint, in others with that of the Codex Alexandrinus; occasionally it seems to correspond with neither, and this has given rise to a theory that he was drawing from a text of the Septuagint different from both of these. Moreover, as it may be doubted whether in the time of Gildas a separate British Latin text had been fully established, the suggestion has been made that he himself knew Greek and translated some of his passages from that language.[82]

This thought of Gildas as intimately acquainted with the Bible brings us naturally to his connection with the British Church. But first it may be well to return for a moment to history.

In what way Christianity was first brought to Britain can now only be matter of conjecture, however probable. No great works or great missionaries stand out in this beginning. We may think that it came little by little, in quiet but sure increase, through the influence of immigrants from Gaul and

[81] See F. C. Burkitt, *Rev. Bénéd.* XLVI, 1934, p. 215.
[82] On all this very difficult question see C. G. Schöll, *De eccles. Britonum Scotorumque hist. fontibus*, p. 17; Haddan and Stubbs, *Councils*, I, p. 175 note, pp. 188ff.; Westcott *s.v. Vulgate* in Smith's *Dict. Bible*, p. 1694; Williams ed. pp. 88f.

of Roman soldiers on duty in Britain. Students of the time no longer believe the story told by Bede and by Nennius that a British King of the second century, Lucius by name, begged Eleutherus, Pope of Rome, to send to Britain teachers of Christian doctrine for himself and his people, and that in response learned prelates came to establish the Mother Sees of London, York, and Caerleon-on-Usk.[33] Nor may we accept without question the testimony of well-known writers to a Britain already Christian early in the third century,[34] even although Tertullian in his work, *Against the Jews,* declares, about 200 A.D., that "places in Britain remote from the Romans are subject to Christ," and Origen, in his sixth Homily on Saint Luke, confesses that "the virtue of the Lord our Saviour is also with those who dwell in Britain apart from our world." [35]

From the third century comes also the story of the death of Britain's first martyr, Saint Alban. Its details were afterward gathered from the dubious sources of some *Acta* or *Passion* of Saint Alban, but the occurrence itself is held true in fact. The names of two other martyrs in early Britain, Aaron and Julius, have come down to us from Caerleon-on-Usk and may also be accepted as authentic. More satisfactory witness to the Christianity of Britain in the fourth century is given by the presence of three British bishops, of York, of London, and, most probably, of Lincoln, at the Council of Arles in 314, proved by their signature below the *Acts* therein enacted, and of others at the Council of Ariminum held in 359.

During the fifth century heresy reared her head in the

---

[33] See Harnack, *Die Mission und Ausbreitung des Christentums,*[4] 1924, II, pp. 884f.; F. E. Warren, *C.M.H.* II, p. 496.

[34] For the original passages see H. Williams, *Christianity in early Britain,* pp. 96ff.; Hadd. and Stubbs, I, pp. 3ff.

[35] *Adv. Jud.* c. 7; ed. Lommatzsch, III, p. 106.

shape of Pelagianism, for which, indeed, Britain seems to have
provided a specially congenial home. Pelagius himself is
thought to have been of British birth; and his comrade in
error, Caelestius, was also of Celtic race, hailing from Ireland.
So grievous was the epidemic of error which ravaged the
Christian body in Britain that two missions were despatched
from Gaul to drive it out. In 429 Germanus, Bishop of
Auxerre, and Lupus, Bishop of Troyes, came, preached, and
conquered, according to the chronicle of Prosper of Aqui-
taine.[36] The fruits of this exhorting were pictured afterward
in the legend of shouts of "Alleluia" from newly converted
soldiers, sending terror into the hearts of the Picts and
Saxons.[37] Once again, in 447, Germanus set out anew,
accompanied this time by Severus, Bishop of Trèves. Further
triumph awaited their arrival. By miracle and by monition
the trouble was cast forth; its promoters were banished from
the island and the Catholic creed firmly established in the
hearts of all.[38]

Already before this time the district of Cumbria, extending
from the Firth of Clyde in Scotland southward over much of
Cumberland and Westmoreland, had been gained for Christianity by the labours of Saint Ninian. In the time of Gildas
the good work he had done was being renewed and furthered
by the pastoral zeal of Saint Kentigern, Bishop of Glasgow,
within this same Cumbria, or Strathclyde, as it is also named.

What, then, does Gildas have to tell us of the history of his
Church in Britain? Some of his omissions are of interest. Not

[36] Mommsen, *Chron. Min.* I, p. 472. For a lively account of both this
mission and the following one see the *Life of Germanus of Auxerre* written
c. 480 by Constantius, the friend of Sidonius Apollinaris, ed. W. Levison,
Script. rer. Merov. VII, pp. 225ff. The subject is fully discussed in Williams, *Christ. in Early Britain*, ch. XIV.
[37] *Vita Germani*, c. 18. On the "Alleluia" story told by Constantius
and afterward by Bede, now regarded as fiction, see Levison, p. 264.
[38] *ibid.* cc. 25ff.

a word of any visit of Saint Paul to Britain, not a word of any mission of Saint Joseph of Arimathea to Glastonbury, not a word of Lucius and the story of his appeal to Rome! Naturally such omissions are not conclusive in themselves; but the silence of Gildas adds its weight to the positive evidence against these legends.

Early in his "mournful letter" he declares that when the true Sun of Christianity rose upon the frost-bound regions of Britain, the gospel of the Church was received but tepidly by the British people. Not till the grievous days of Diocletian, according to this record, did the Church in Britain attain any special glory; when "of a free gift in the time, so it seems, of the persecution, the Lord lighted for us the radiant lamps of the holy martyrs lest Britain should be hid utterly in the dense fog of dark night. Even now, the places where they suffered and where their bodies were buried would still kindle no little fire of divine charity in the hearts of those gazing at them, if these had not been taken from us, not so much by sad pillage of barbarians as by our own many crimes. I am referring to holy Alban of Verulamium, and to Aaron and Julius of the City of the Legions,[39] and the other citizens of either sex who in different places with high courage stood firm in the battle field of Christ." [40]

There follows the story of the death of Alban:

"Through love he followed the example of Christ Who laid down His life for the sheep. For he rescued a confessor from capture by enemies of the faith; first, by hiding him in his own home and afterward by exchange of clothing. In this brother's dress he freely gave himself to the peril of pursuit;

[39] Caerleon-on-Usk.
[40] Some scholars maintain that the persecution should be held that of Decius or of Valerian, as that of Diocletian is not known to have included Britain; cf. Williams, *Christianity in Early Britain*, p. 109; Haddan and Stubbs, I, p. 6.

and being found well-pleasing to God by his holy witness and the shedding of his blood, he was honoured marvellously by signs and wonders in the presence of those impious men who carried the Roman standards with dreadful pride. By power of prayer he opened up a mysterious way across the bed of the noble river Thames, walking with a thousand men on dry feet while the whirling waters rose sheer on either side; like that road of the Israelites, also dry but less worn, where the ark of the Covenant stood long on the pebbles in the midst of Jordan. Then Alban changed the first of the executioners awaiting him from a wolf into a lamb by the sight of such wonders and made him, too, athirst for the triumphant palm of martyrdom." [41]

Here is our earliest authority for the place and period at which Alban suffered. Of course Gildas, who did not know the east of Britain well, is wrong in calling the river the Thames; he is really referring to the little stream, the Ver, which would have easily yielded a crossing to this eager Christian. Even before the time of Gildas the priest Constantius had told how Germanus and Lupus had visited the tomb of Saint Alban and offered thanksgiving there.[42] Other sure witness for the veneration of Alban in the sixth century is given by Venantius Fortunatus, who writes in his poem on *Virginity:*

"Glorious Alban comes from fertile Britain." [43]

To the Venerable Bede we owe our second account of Alban, much enlarged by other material, found probably in some *Acta.* He gives the day of Alban's death as June 22, on which it is set

[41] cc. 10f.
[42] *Vita Germani,* 16. For accretions in the story as given by Bede, see W. Meyer, *Abh. d. König. Gesell. d. Wiss. zu Gött., Phil. hist. Kl.* N.F. VIII, 1904, pp. 1ff.
[43] *Carm.* VIII, iii, 155.

for commemoration in the Roman Church, though the Anglican Book of Common Prayer has chosen June 17.[44] Later *Acta* of Saint Alban give much legend, but nothing of proven fact. Of Aaron and Julius we know no more than is told us here and in Bede, drawing on Gildas, except that there is a mention in the *Book of Llan Dav* of a "merthyr" or "place of martyrdom" of Julius and Aaron near Caerleon-on-Usk.[45]

About ten years later, Gildas goes on to say, when the force of persecution had been spent, light returned to Britain as if after a long dark winter night. Then men rebuilt the churches which had been levelled to the ground, founded new shrines in honour of holy martyrs, and celebrated the feast days of the Catholic religion with joyful hearts and pure lips. Such a happy state of peace continued till "the Arian treachery, as a savage serpent, vomited forth its poison from overseas upon us in Britain, causing fatal separation among brethren who had dwelt in unity. Then, just as though a road had been made across the ocean, all the fierce beasts of every kind of heresy, quivering their deadly fangs, planted wounds into my country, that ever longed to hear something new and held nothing fast." It is interesting, however, that Gildas says nothing of Pelagianism. Can we believe it was dead in this Britain of the sixth century, healed and purified by the campaigns of Germanus and his fellow-Bishops?

Other evils, however, and perhaps worse than heresy, were found by Gildas in the Church of his own day. When he has ended his rebuke of the kings of Britain, he turns to denounce as fiercely her priests, as one of their own number.[46] Some, it is true, are glorious in their holy lives. But so great and of

[44] In the proposed book of 1928 the date was changed to June 22.
[45] Williams, ed. p. 27, followed by Baring-Gould and Fisher, I, pp. 101ff.
[46] See F. E. Warren, *Liturgy and Ritual of the Celtic Church*, p. 69.

such kind are the wickednesses of bishops and of priests and of clerics of his own (monastic) vocation that he must speak his mind for their eternal good. Wherefore, "with my sides protected against defeat by the shields of saints, and my back stayed against the walls of truth, and my head covered as with a helmet by the aid of the Lord, let the stones of my angry words fly thick and fast in truthful assault." These may better be read in his text.

Later on we find passages drawn from Lessons appointed to be read in the Office of the British Church for the Ordination of Priests, quoted by Gildas in order that the guilty ministers may be reminded of the injunctions laid upon them in the very day of the laying on of hands. These Lessons of the British Ordinal differ from those appointed in other parts of the Western Church.[47] Of greater interest is the mention of anointing of the hands as part of the ritual of ordination: "I have considered it necessary to refer to those Lessons which have been carefully selected from every pertinent text of the Holy Scriptures; not only for the sake of my own purpose, but for their approving of the consecration by which the hands of priests and deacons [or "of priests or ministers"] are initiated." [48] As early, then, as the sixth century the anointing of the hands of priests at ordination was practised in the British Church, whence it has been thought that the custom found place in the Anglo-Saxon and the Gallican Churches.[49] In the Anglo-Saxon Pontifical which represents the usage about the time of Egbert, Archbishop of York in

[47] cc. 64ff.
[48] The words of Gildas here are: *qua initiantur sacerdotum vel ministrorum manus.* The word *vel* sometimes means "and" in Latin of this period, and not improbably may be so understood here. See Duchesne, *Christian Worship,*[5] p. 370 note. Williams, ed. p. 239, translates "of priests or ministers," and thinks that *ministri* may mean "deacons," but probably also means "priests."
[49] Duchesne, *ibid.* p. 378; Maskell, *Monumenta Ritualia Ecclesiae Anglicanae,* II[2], pp. CXXIIf.; p. 224.

the eighth century, we find directions for the consecrating with holy oil and chrism of the hands of those ordained to Holy Orders. The prayer said by the Bishop at the anointing of those ordained priest runs in translation:

"Bless, O Lord, and sanctify these hands of this Thy Priest unto the consecrating of the Hosts which are offered for the sins and negligences of the people, and unto other blessings which they shall need. And grant, we beseech, that whatsoever they have blessed may be blessed and whatsoever they hallow may be hallowed: O Saviour of the world, Who livest and reignest. . . ." Then the Bishop made the sign of the Cross with holy chrism over the hands of the newly ordained priest and added a further prayer: "May these hands, we beseech Thee, O Lord, be consecrated and sanctified by this holy anointing and our invocation and the divine benediction, that whatsoever they have blessed may be blessed and whatsoever they have sanctified may be sanctified. Through. . . ." [50]

In the *Missale Francorum* of the Gallican Church this same prayer is found, with an alternative form, beginning:

"May these hands be anointed with hallowed oil and the chrism of sanctification. Even as Samuel anointed David as King and Prophet, so may they be anointed. . . ." [51] Three ancient Gallican sacramentaries of the tenth century, published by Martène, order this same anointing, with the prayer *Consecrentur manus istae,* [52] very similar to that used in the Roman Church at the present day, when the Bishop blesses the hands of those ordained priest with the sign of the Cross in holy oil. The ceremony of anointing was omitted in English mediaeval Orderings and in the English Ordinal composed from them in 1549-1550.

[50] Martène, *De antiquis ecclesiae ritibus,* Tom. 2, 1763, pp. 31ff.
[51] Muratori, *Liturgia Romana vetus,* II, 1748, p. 669.
[52] *ibid.* p. 44.

The tradition seems not to have been practised in early times at Rome. In 864 Pope Nicolas the first, in answer to an enquiry from Rodulph, Archbishop of Bourges, on this matter of anointing in ordination, wrote definitely that neither for those ordained priest or deacon was this the custom in the Church of Rome at his time.[53] This statement has been contrasted with two others from Churchmen of Gaul in the ninth century: Amalarius of Metz, pupil of Alcuin, who declares that bishops anoint with oil the hands of priests in remembrance of the sons of Aaron, that they may with purity offer the Holy Sacrifice;[54] and Theodulph, Bishop of Orleans, who charges his clergy to be mindful of the anointing of their hands at ordination.[55]

The custom, therefore, was apparently British and Gallican at this time, not Roman.

We come now to the story of the life of Gildas, a matter very largely overgrown with legend of later centuries. There are two "Lives" written of him. One, by Vitalis, a monk of the Monastery of Rhuis in Brittany, dates probably from the eleventh century and incorporates material composed far earlier.[56] The second is printed under the name of Carodoc of Llancarfan, friend of Geoffrey of Monmouth, and, if this attribution is correct, must belong to the twelfth century. That Gildas was especially acquainted with Western Britain is shown in his "Querulous History" by his mention of the Battle of Badon Hill and his rebukes of the Five Kings in the West. Vitalis describes him as receiving his early training in

---

[53] *PL* CXIX, 884.
[54] *De ecclesiasticis officiis,* II, 13: *PL* CV, 1089.
[55] *Capitula ad presbyteros parochiae suae: PL* CV, 192f.
[56] Both *Lives* are printed with trans. and introd. by Williams in his edition, pp. 317ff. *Vita I* was first published in 1605 by John à Bosco in his *Bibliotheca Floriacensis,* and was reproduced in the Bollandist edition: *Acta* SS. Jan. 29. *Vita II* was first published by Stevenson in his edition made for the English Historical Society in 1838.

the famous monastic School founded by Illtyd in South Wales.

The mediaeval *Life* of this Founder [57] states that he was born in Brittany, that his father was a Breton noble and his mother a daughter of one of the British kings. We are told that he became a soldier and crossed to England to stay a while in the court of King Arthur of Britain, who was his cousin. From there he travelled on with his wife Trynihid to Glamorgan and its King Paulinus, who made him Commander of all its army.

One day he went on a hunting expedition with the officers of the royal Palace. When it was time for the midday meal, they found themselves near the cloister presided over by the great Cadoc, and sent a haughty message to the Saint that he should make haste to prepare dinner. So he did. But the Lord took away from them all power of eating it, and as they sat helplessly facing the food, the earth suddenly opened and swallowed them alive.

Not quite all, however. Illtyd had been busy in another part of the forest when these dreadful things occurred and was so overcome by their terror that he humbly approached Saint Cadoc and begged for instruction. Instruction led to conversion, and the soldier henceforth was lost in the hermit. With his wife and a few serving-men he wandered through Glamorgan, till at length, in a hut hastily built of reeds by the side of the River Daw, he dreamed in a vision of an Angel who bade him forsake the world with its bonds and seek a certain valley surrounded by many trees. He promptly set out, "vehemently repenting that he had ever loved his wife of the flesh," and finally settled down in the valley called Hodnant, "the Fertile Dale," delightful with wooded slopes

---

[57] W. J. Rees, *Lives of the Cambro-British Saints*, pp. 465ff ; also an abridged form in *Nova Legenda Anglie*, II, pp. 52ff.

shadowing a pleasant stream. There, on the banks of the river, Illtyd built a little church in honour of the most High and Undivided Trinity, in which he fasted and prayed night and day.

He was not allowed to remain long in solitude. Shortly afterward Meirchion, King of Glamorgan, happened to pass this retreat while out hunting and took the edge off a keen appetite with a meagre lunch of fish and water from its brook. The story goes on that he found this unaccustomed repast excellent and then and there in a mellow mood gave Illtyd permission to establish a permanent home in this valley and to exercise some kind of rule over all its region. Also, said the King, it would be well if Illtyd shared his love of prayer and holy discipline with others. Let him establish there a School for those who craved to learn and practise things of the spirit. The Saint obeyed this call and "there flocked to him very many disciples, among them four scholars of note, Samson and Paul and Gildas and David, with more even as they." [58]

So Illtyd became Abbot of a monastery, and his pupils in the course of years began to attain fame. Brittany desired Samson as Bishop of Dol. The prayer was granted, and the Cathedral of Saint Samson still marks his presence in this charming little Breton town about fourteen miles from St. Malo. Another ancient town, St. Pol-de-Léon, near Morlaix, commemorates Paul Aurelianus, who settled in the district of Léon and was consecrated its Bishop. His relics are still honoured in the Cathedral at the annual Pardon, and the site of his tomb is still pointed out before its high altar. Of the third of these Saints, Dewi or David, we read that he went on from the School of Illtyd to another place of monastic training almost as famous, founded, according to tradition,

[58] Cf. a similar statement in the *Life* of Paulinus (Paulus Aurelianus), dated 884; *Anal. Boll.* I (1882) p. 215. But it is not certain that David was one of the company of Illtyd: Lloyd, *Hist. of Wales*, I, p. 144.

by Saint Paulinus at Ty-gwyn (Whitland) in Carmarthen.[59] Afterward he founded his own monastery, known in later days as the school of Menevia, and, as its Abbot, spread through Wales the glory of that place, now known to us as St. David's. There the Cathedral with its dignified beauty fitly perpetuates his name.

These were the companions, so record tells, who shared with Gildas the lessons given by Illtyd in his School of the Hodnant. Its site is usually thought to be Llantwit Major, that delightful village in the Vale of Glamorgan some eighteen miles from Cardiff, known to the Welsh in former days as Llanilltyd Fawr. The river that runs near is still called the Odnant, and a mile or so away the sea beats on rocks and cliffs. Its white-washed cottages stand in picturesque streets around the old Town Hall, where a tiny tower bears still on its bell the prayer *Sancte Illtute, ora pro nobis*. All that surrounds the modern pilgrim to this shrine of holiness and learning still wears the mark of days long gone: the *Old Hart Inn* with its floors and roofs fashioned many centuries ago; the *Old Swan Inn* with its gabled front; Plymouth House, built according to tradition where the School of Illtyd once had its home. One can still imagine ancient monastic dwellings where now only ruins can be seen. An old gravelled lane leads down to the church of Saint Illtyd, beautiful within and without. Outside, in the midst of a wealth of pink and red roses which hang over and between the graves in this churchyard during the summer months of pilgrimage, there stand a Preaching Cross of great antiquity and the ruins of a Galilee Chapel. Within, the church is divided into two parts, western and eastern. The eastern portion is of interest for its Jesse Niche and its old frescoes, to say nothing of its fair and decent

[59] There is no ancient evidence that Paulinus founded his school exactly at Whitland: Lloyd, *ibid.* p. 151.

modern adornment. The western part, now unused for service, holds ancient monuments and especially draws students of Gildas and his times for its Celtic Cross, dating probably from the ninth or tenth century. On it scholarship has faintly discerned the name of Illtyd. The name is certainly visible to all on a stone slab set up hard by in memory of an Illtyd who lived in the seventeenth century, and it has been borne by sons of the village down the years. The present church dates in general from the thirteenth century; but it is good to imagine that one stands in it on the place where Illtyd and his students once offered their Eucharist.

It is possible, however, that Illtyd founded more than one monastic settlement, as his *Life* represents him dwelling with his disciples on "a certain narrow little island rough and dry of soil." From this, together with other mediaeval traditions, the theory has arisen that Illtyd's monastery was situated on Caldey Island, the ancient Ynys Pyr, off the coast of Pembroke. The island is still the home of monks at the present day and still acknowledges Saint Samson as its patron. Among the buildings once owned by the Caldey Benedictines is a Priory built in the twelfth and thirteenth centuries, re-dedicated by them to St. Illtyd, with a window of stained glass in his honour. Whether Illtyd founded both monasteries or not, it is certain that both have come down to us in close connection with his name.[60] That name stands in Celtic monasticism with those of either Finnian; of the "Twelve Apostles of Erin," once disciples under Finnian of Clonard; of the three of this company best known among men, Ciaran

[60] See Lloyd, pp. 144f.; Williams, ed. pp. 332t.; *Christ. in Early Britain*, pp. 322ff.; *Lives* of St. Samson (*Anal. Boll.* VI, p. 93), St. Paulus (*ibid.* I, pp. 213ff.) and Gildas (*Vita* I, c. 4); Giraldus Cambrensis (*Rer. Brit. medii aevi Script.*) VI, p. 92. Williams suggests that the original monastery of Illtyd on Caldey Island was afterward thought wrongly to have been located at Llantwit Major. But the *Vita Samsonis* speaks of the "island" as "not far from" the monastery of Illtyd.

of Clonmacnoise, Brendan of Clonfert, Columba of Iona.
With these we shall tarry a little while when we come to think
more specially of Irish cloisters in the sixth century. But we
are not to forget that in this great record the names of saints
of Wales stand out in all their own brilliance: of Illtyd; of
Cadoc, Abbot of Llancarfan; of Dubricius and Teilo and
Oudoceus; of David and of Deiniol.

We are told that from time to time the School of Illtyd was
visited by the Bishop Dubricius, especially in the season of
Lent, that he might approve its doings and correct what
needed amendment.[61] The statement savours of a later day.
In this sixth century of the Celtic Church its bishops, both in
Britain and in Ireland, were predominantly monastic, attached
to monasteries for the conferring of Holy Orders, under the
jurisdiction of abbots, rather than rulers of Sees and Visitors
vested with authority.[62] Under Illtyd, then, this monastic
School so flourished that it continued for many years to be
a centre of learning for students of doctrine both ecclesiastical
and secular, until its work passed to the mediaeval universities.

The date of the birth of Gildas is given in his own statement as the same as that of the battle of Badon Hill. But
around the year of that battle much tide of controversy has
swirled. The actual words of Gildas are: "From this time
onward, now our citizens, now the enemy were victorious . . .
until the year of the siege of Badon Hill and almost the last
important blow dealt to the [Saxon] rascals. Here, to my own
knowledge, begins the forty-fourth year, with one month
already gone, and this is also the year of my own birth." [63]
Does this mean, as Bede thought it did, the forty-fourth year
after the coming of the Saxon enemy to Britain? In that case

[61] *Life* of St. Dubricius, *Liber Landavensis*, p. 78.
[62] See Lloyd, I, pp. 156f.; Willis Bund, *The Celtic Church of Wales*,
c. V.
[63] c. 26.

the date, 516, given by the *Annales Cambriae* for the battle, must certainly be wrong.[64] Mommsen, however, understands that Gildas is stating that at the time of his present writing forty-three years and one month have passed since the year of the battle and the year of his birth.[65] Now we have seen that Maelgwn, King in Northern Wales, died about 547, and Gildas rebukes him as one still living. Therefore Gildas must have been writing not far from this time. As he makes no mention of the Yellow Plague which carried off Maelgwn, it is possible that he was writing a little before 547. In that case the year of Gildas's birth would be shortly after 500, a date which is rendered not unlikely by the mention of his death in the *Annales Cambriae* in 570.[66]

Legend has given us a pleasant glimpse of him and his companions in Llantwit Major. It tells that sea-gulls kept on swooping down upon the early harvest of grain in the fields around the monastery till Illtyd divided out the work of keeping guard among his young novices day by day. Once, when it happened to be Paul's day for the watch, he was assailed by a specially large flock; although he ran up and down and shouted himself hoarse, he could not keep them from settling on the juicy shoots of the springing corn. So he called the other boys, Gildas and Samson, to help him, and as they tore wildly after the gulls, they besought aid of the Lord. Their faith was rewarded; all the screaming, swooping crowd were suddenly driven together as if they

[64] See Bede, *H.E.* I, 16 and Plummer's note thereon; Zimmer, *Nenn. Vind.* pp. 100; 286f.; A. de la Borderie, *Revue Celtique*, VI, pp. 1ff.; *Annales Cambriae*, p. 830.

[65] ed. p. 8. He amends the passage thus: *quique quadragesimus quartus (est ab eo qui) orditur annus mense iam uno emenso, qui et meae nativitatis est.* Another emendation of *quia* for *qui* is easier and yields equally good result: see the discussion by J. N. L. Myres, *Roman Britain*, pp. 46of.

[66] p. 831. Myres, however, points out the difficulty of trusting the *Annales* for the dates 547 and 570 and refusing to accept that of 516.

were sheep, not wild birds, right into the monastery Chapel where the Father was praying. Even his detachment was not proof against their angry shrieks, and he bade the boys release them, in the sure belief that they would never again dare to molest the harvest of the monks.

Later on the tradition of Gildas crosses the sea and makes him Abbot of a monastery he himself founded in southern Brittany, in the district of the present village of Saint Gildas-de-Rhuis, about twenty miles from Vannes in the Morbihan. There a beautiful Romanesque Church stands on the site of the old abbey, still named in honour of Saint Gildas and still preserving his tomb behind the high altar. We find there, also, a modern statue of the Saint, with his Abbot's staff in his left hand and his right raised in blessing. At his feet fresh flowers show the reverence with which he is honoured; tablets from grateful pilgrims record the gifts granted by his intercession, and litanies rest by his shrine for the recitation of those who believe in the Communion of Saints:

> Saint Gildas, who drank no wine nor other strong drink,
> Saint Gildas, who brought to nought the artifices of demons,
> Saint Gildas, who wrought miracles by your prayers:
>> Pray for us.

A golden case holds a relic, and the Saint's Feast is commemorated yearly on the twenty-ninth of January, held as the day of his death.

From the church we turn to the road and walk along the cliffs with a glorious view of sea and coast till we reach the Grand-Mont and climb down by steps into a little cove. Half-way down we come upon a statue of Gildas in gray stone, standing out against the rock ferns and the pink sea-thrift. At its feet lies a pool of clear water, the "Good Fountain." Below, the sea breaks against the shore, and further out, past a tiny fishing-boat or two, picturesque with red sails, we discover the Île-de-Houat, to which Gildas is said to have retired for solitary meditation and prayer. A story tells that he was miraculously transported by a leap of his horse from this very spot, and even the print of the horse's hoof is still pointed out on the rock near at hand!

Did Gildas live here in retreat while Breton history waxed fierce and violent? It was during this period and in this very neighbourhood that Chramn, son of Chlotar the first, King of the Franks, fled from his father's rage to the protection of Chanao, Count of Vannes. Not far off Chanao was killed by Chlotar and Chramn was captured; we have seen his terrible ending in the story of Gregory of Tours.[67] But in the *Complaint on the ruin of Britain* we read nothing of the miseries of this lesser Britain across the Channel, and the question where it was written still remains undecided. It would be interesting if we might think of him in the cloister where centuries afterward Abelard was to ponder on the problems of scholastic philosophy, as Abbot of a monastery now fallen on evil times, while he sought brief solace from the trials and troubles with which his unruly monks for nearly ten years vexed his soul.[68]

Other places in Brittany still keep Gildas in mind. Locminé, near Vannes, holds his statue, and Churches at Auray and at Saint-Gildas-des-Bois in the same part of the country are dedicated in his name. At Castennac on the bank of the River Blavet near Pontivy the Grotto of Saint Gildas recalls the tradition, given in his *Life,* that he built a chapel here under the jutting rock.[69] A stone that gives out a ringing sound when struck is said to have been used by him to mark the hour of prayer.

---

[67] *Hist. Franc.* IV, c. 20.
[68] But see my notes 73 and 79.

[69] *Vita* I, c. 17.

Record tells further that Gildas journeyed to Ireland and spent some time there in preaching. It is not necessary, at any rate, to believe that he sent a gift to Saint Brigid, as the first *Life* states.[70] There is other evidence from the same *Life* in mention of a request for his help as missionary from King Ainmire of Ireland, and the traditional date of Ainmire's reign, about 565, fits in well.[71] Another ancient tradition states that Gildas, together with David, gave a Liturgy of the Mass to the Second Order of Irish Saints, in existence during this same century.[72]

What, we ask, is of truth in all these stories? It is impossible to draw the line exactly. The careful sifting of Ferdinand Lot leaves us with few grains of result: the birth of Gildas about 500, a life mainly spent in South-West Britain, journeys to Ireland and to Brittany, perhaps in flight from his wrathful "tyrants," and death, possibly in Ireland.[73]

And now there open out before us yet other fields of legend, still more thickly grown with myth. After all, legend presents a charming view.

The first *Life,* then, declares that Gildas was born of a chieftain named Caunus in the district of the Clyde, and the place may be correct. The traditional equivalent of Caunus in Welsh is Caw.[74] Caw, according to the monk of Rhuis, who compiled this first *Life,* had five children, and, of these, three sons and the only daughter embraced the monastic vocation. There is a pleasant story that two of these brothers with their sister went to live in a lonely part of the country,

[70] Williams, ed. pp. 338f.; *Vita* I, c. 10.

[71] *Vita* I, cc. 11f. The *Annals of Ulster* date the accession of Ainmire in 565 and his slaying in 568 or 575: ed. W. M. Hennessy, I, 1887, pp. 6off.

[72] Haddan and Stubbs, II, p. 292f.

[73] *Mélanges d'histoire bretonne,* 1907, pp. 265f.; *Medieval Studies in memory of G. S. Loomis,* 1927, p. 262. The words *transmarina relatio* applied by Gildas to continental writings (*De exc.* c. 4) seem to oppose the theory that he wrote his *Complaint* in Brittany: Lot, *Mél.* p. 252, note 2.

[74] Williams, ed. p. 323.

where the young men, who evidently had been ordained to the priesthood, built three little places of prayer, one for each, placing their sister's cell in the middle between them. Each day one of the brothers in turn shared his Mass and his daily Offices with her, supping with her after Vespers and then, with a last thanksgiving, returning to his own hut before sundown. All their years the three continued thus and were buried where they had lived and prayed.[75]

We read, too, that Gildas travelled to Rome to honour the shrines of its saints and to Ravenna to beg the intercession of holy Apollinaris, revered in the Cathedral of that city. In Rome he is said to have slain in the Name of Christ a horrible dragon that was poisoning many people by its breath.[76] Moreover, he presented a splendid gift to the Pope. It is said that he had once paid a visit by night to Saint Cadoc, at the monastic School of Llancarfan which Cadoc had founded about five miles from Llantwit Major. With him he brought a bell, made by himself, so wonderful in its beauty and the sweetness of its sound that Cadoc begged Gildas to sell it to him, even going so far as to offer to fill it full of gold as its price. But Gildas steadily refused to part with his work, destined as an offering to God and Saint Peter at Rome. It was duly presented to the Holy Father, who received it with much joy. But when the Pope had admired its exquisite art and struck the bell to hear its note, not a sound would it utter! Gildas protested that it had made very sweet music for Cadoc. "Cadoc?" said the Pope. "I know him well. Seven times has he journeyed here on pilgrimage and thrice to Jerusalem, begging mercy of the Lord for the souls of his family and friends. Let the holy man have the bell with my blessing, and let it be revered by all the British as a refuge from evil. Let them swear on it and truly. Whosoever shall swear falsely on this bell and shall

[75] *Vita* I, c. 2.   [76] *ibid.* cc. 13ff.

not repent, without doubt he shall lie under a curse." The bell was returned to Llancarfan and promptly gave out marvellous sounds, "like to the voices of angels." [77]

Another story relates that Cadoc asked his friend Gildas to be master of the school at Llancarfan for a year, and that he did so without asking any fee in return except the prayers of its clergy and its students. During this time he is said to have copied out the Four Gospels; and men in Wales of a later day, according to tradition, made oath upon this Book as a sacred heritage. When the year had ended, Cadoc and Gildas decided to go into retreat, and chose the two islands in the Bristol Channel, then known as Ronech and Echni, but now called the Steep Holme and the Flat Holme. [78] Gildas retired to the island "nearer England," the Steep Holme, which one sees plainly in walking along the sea-front at Weston-super-Mare. Steamers carry visitors over the five miles which lie between it and the town. It is only a mile or so in area, but holds great interest for botanists in its rare varieties of wild flowers. There Gildas sat, if the legend be true, and meditated in some one of its many caves while the countless seabirds wailed above his head. He lived on the eggs he took from their nests and on little fish which he caught in a net; his bed was a rock lying under the cliff, and on it he knelt in prayer till midnight, chilled to the bone. Close by he built a chapel, once more in the Name of the Holy Trinity, and here he spent the rest of his night when the cold drove him within. [79]

[77] *Vita* II, cc. 6f.; also in *Life of St. Cadoc:* see Rees, *Cambro-British Saints*, pp. 58ff.

[78] *Vita* II, c. 9. Cf. *Life of St. Oudoceus, Liber Landavensis*, ed. Rees, p. 131; *Life of St. Cadoc*, p. 66.

[79] See Lot (*Mél.* p. 266, note 1) and Wade-Evans (*Welsh Christian Origins*, pp. 239f.) for the suggestion of the island of Echni as the place of composition of the *Complaint of Gildas*. The names Ronech and Echni are found interchanged in our authorities.

Statues or pictures of Gildas usually place a bell by his side because of his fame as artist in metal-work. A bell was said to have been his present to Saint Brigid of Ireland, and a story very like that of Gildas and the Pope represents him as giving another to his former Abbot, Saint Illtyd. The *Life* of Illtyd tells that he was not allowed to live out his days in peace in his happy vale, the Hodnant, but was much troubled by the insults and accusations thrown against him by a certain steward of King Meirchion. At last he could stand it no longer, and retreated in fear for his life to a hidden cave near the River Ewenny. One day a messenger passed by, bearing a bell made by Gildas as a gift from him to Saint David at Menevia. Illtyd longed for the bell, and was refused; David, however, like the Pope before him, could strike no sound, and Illtyd finally rejoiced in its beauty. So, we are sure, did the angels, who are said to have encouraged the exile in his cave by the stream.[80]

The mediaeval *Life of Saint David* tells a story different from the one we have noted, of David and Gildas as boys together under Illtyd. We read here that the father of David, King Sandde of Wales, had violated a nun. Her name was Nonn, and she was very beautiful and innocent of evil. Shortly before her child was born, she went into church, partly to make accustomed offerings and prayers that she might be safely delivered, partly to hear the preaching of Saint Gildas. Directly she entered, Gildas fell silent, just as though his throat were closed. The congregation asked him why he thus suddenly stopped his sermon, and he answered: "I can still speak to you in commonplace words, but I can no longer preach. Go ye without and leave me here alone that I may see if so I may be able to preach." All the people walked out except the woman pregnant with

[80] *Life of St. Illtyd:* Rees, *Cambro-British Saints*, p. 175.

child, who hid herself in a corner, not because of wilful disobedience, but because of her great need of help in this hour. Then again Gildas tried with all his might and main to start his sermon, but never a word would come. At length in terror he cried aloud: "I adjure thee, come forth, if there be any one hiding here!" So the woman answered: "I am hiding here between the door and the wall." Then Gildas understood, and told her to go out and bid the people come in again. All trooped in, wild with curiosity, and took their places as before. Gildas preached loud and clear as a trumpet, but gave no explanation till his sermon had ended. Then he called in the woman from outside and declared solemnly: "The son to be born of this holy mother has a greater grace and power and calling than I, because God has given to him privilege and rule over all the saints of Britain for ever." Such words of prophecy greeted the coming of David, and from that time Gildas refused to minister any longer to the British people.[81] Another version of the story tells that the sermon was given on a Sunday, as Gildas preached always on this day in church by the sea in the district of Pepidiauc.[82]

Another marvel regarding the birth of a child is related as having happened while Gildas was in Brittany. There was a Breton chieftain named Chonomor, of whom Gregory of Tours tells that he saved Macliav, afterward Bishop of Vannes, from the fury of Chanao, whom we have seen as Count of that place. Macliav was brother of Chanao, and Chanao seems to have had a consuming desire to murder all his male kin. Therefore Chonomor hid Macliav in a hole underground and told his pursuer he was dead.[83] In the first *Life* of Gildas Chonomor appears far differently, as a brutal tyrant who made a practice of slaying each wife he mar-

---

[81] Rees, *ibid.* pp. 119ff.
[82] In South Wales: *Vita* II, c. 4.
[83] *Hist. Franc.* IV, 4.

ried, and of these there were many, directly she gave promise of bearing a child. Finally no decent man would have anything to say to him, and the Abbot Gildas refused to hearken to any request he made. Presently he was seized, as the tale goes, by a desire to wed the daughter of Weroc, another Count of Vannes, who declared that nothing on this earth could induce him to give his daughter to a murderer. Chonomor protested that he would hand over any security the father wished as guarantee of his honourable intentions, and Weroc at last consented, provided that Gildas would promise assurance for her safety. After some hesitation the Abbot decided to trust in the Lord and do as he was asked.

All happened as many times before. The young bride, at first cherished tenderly, lost all her husband's affection directly she was with child, and Chonomor again meditated murder. For a long time the fear of Gildas held him back, till his wife, terrified by ominous signs of her coming fate, fled from husband and home. This decided the matter. Chonomor rushed in pursuit, found her lying under a hedge by the roadside half-dead with the toils of her flight, and completed the process by cutting off her head.

Naturally the enraged father heaped reproaches on Gildas. But he was equal even to this occasion. In boiling indignation he hastened to a small fortress where Chonomor was residing, only to find the doors locked against him and the guards jeering at his demand for entrance. When he grew tired of knocking, he fell to prayer and then threw a handful of earth on the building. At once by the will of God it collapsed. Then the holy man hurried off to find the dead body of the girl, still lying by the road. Again a prayer to the Lord and Giver of life, and lo! the maid rose up and obeyed his bidding to tell what she had seen after death: "I was carried directly by angels to join the throng of mar-

tyrs, but then you called me to come back." Gildas delivered her to her father, and she bore a son, whom he caused
to be baptized and named after himself. The mother entered
a convent afterward, but the boy grew up to be a saint.
The Bretons called him Trechmor, and he and his mother,
whose name was Triphina, are still to be found in the calendar of Saints honoured at Carhaix, where the murder was
said to have been done. Trechmor is patron of the town,
and its church is dedicated in due honour to Saint Trémeur.
Under the arcade of the West Door his statue pictures him
as a young man, holding his head in his hands. For the story
twists and turns in various shapes, and a second version states
that Chonomor murdered young Trechmor, son of his wife
Triphina by another man.[84]

Among all these shifting currents of legend we find the
tale that Gildas dwelt for long at Glastonbury, and wish we
could accept it as William of Malmesbury did. In his book
on *The Ancient Church of Glastonbury* he tells that "Gildas,
an historian neither stupid nor dull, to whom the Britons
owe any notice that other nations take of them, spent many
years here, fascinated by the holiness of the place. And here
in 512 he departed this life and was buried in the ancient
church before the altar." [85] It was pleasant, of course, for
those who loved Glastonbury to believe that Gildas, too, the
British historian and holy man, as well as Patrick and Brigid
and David, had journeyed to this "home of the Saints."
Caradoc, a contemporary of William, also writes of Gildas
in Glastonbury.[86] By him we are told that Gildas was forced
to leave his retreat on the Steep Holme because pirates from

[84] *Vita* I, cc. 20ff.; *The Book of Saints* by the Benedictines of S. Augustine's Abbey, Ramsgate, 3rd ed. 1934, *s.v. Tremorus;* Holweck, *Biographi-
cal Dictionary of the Saints,* pp. 988f.
[85] Adam of Domerham, *Hist. Glast.* ed. Hearne, 1727, p. 18.
[86] *Vita* II, cc. 10ff.

the Orkney Islands carried off his servants and his furniture, rather strange appurtenances for an austere hermit! Then he climbed into a little boat and came to Glastonbury, sad at heart. Its Abbot welcomed him, and he settled down to teach both the monks and lay people the truths of heavenly doctrine. And in Glastonbury, we read, he composed a "History of the Kings of Britain." During his life there "Glastonbury was besieged by King Arthur with an innumerable host, for that Guinevere his wife had been captured . . . and had been brought there for safe-keeping, to a place that had never been surprised on account of its protection by reed-thickets and river and marsh. The angry King had sought his Queen for the space of a whole year and at length had learned of her abode. At once he stirred up the armies of all Cornubia and Dibnenia and war was made ready between enemies.

"At this the Abbot of Glastonbury with his clergy and Gildas the Wise intervened between the two lines and counselled Melvas their King to make peace and restore his captive. So she was restored, as was meet, in peace and goodwill." The story goes on that the two Kings gave broad lands to the Abbot and prayed in the Church of Saint Mary, promising to obey reverently the Abbot of Glastonbury and never to violate this most holy place nor even the region adjacent thereto.

Then Gildas conceived the desire of living as a hermit on the bank of the river near at hand and built a church in the Name of the Holy and Undivided Trinity. There he fasted and prayed, clad in a habit of goat's hair, and many pilgrims came to visit him from distant parts of Britain for the joy of his counsel. There he died, and was buried with right worthy honour and great mourning in the centre of the pavement of the Church of Saint Mary.

Yet another narrative is given by the monk of Rhuis in the first *Life*.[87] He declares that the time of his departure was revealed as imminent to Gildas by an angel in a dream, when he was sleeping one night in the Île-de-Houat. For a week he lived on, admonishing and encouraging his disciples with his last words. Then on the eighth day he bade them carry him into his little chapel, where he received the Viaticum of the Lord's Body and charged the brethren to place him after his death in a ship, with his head resting on the stone on which he used to sleep. None should stay with him, but they were to push off the ship and let it go forth into the sea, whither God should will. "For," he ended, "I trust in the Lord that in the Day of Resurrection He will make me to rise with the rest. And now the God of peace and love be ever with you all."

Thus he died, on the 29th of January, according to our biographer, an old man and full of days. His disciples did as he had desired them and placed him on a ship; whereupon others, and these were many, brethren from Cornugallia,[88] attempted to carry off his body to his own country of Britain. While these were trying to do this, by the will of God the ship sank with its holy burden into the depth of the sea! For long they searched here and there, but to no purpose, and were finally obliged to return in disappointment to their homes.

But the faithful disciples from the monastery of Rhuis sought diligently for three months, and when all their efforts, also, were fruitless, they decided to offer three days of fasting and prayer for their desire. When, therefore, the "Rogation Days" had come, and it seems possible that in the legend they were actually those appointed by the Church in the fifth century, for the month was now May, the brethren found

[87] cc. 28ff.   [88] Cornouailles in Brittany.

the body safe and unhurt in the ship where they had placed it, standing in an inlet of the coast called the Cove of the Holy Cross. With great rejoicing they laid the stone which had served as pillow upon an altar in that place and bore the body itself back to the church at Rhuis. Ever since that time, declares the monk, this day, the eleventh of May, has been observed as a Feast among the people of Vannes. At the present day, indeed, the solemnity of the Translation of the relics of Saint Gildas is kept on May 11 in this diocese, as well as that of his death on January 29.

Enough of legend. We will turn lastly for a glance at certain other writings of Gildas, more interesting in some ways than his tearful *Complaint*. A few words will suffice for the *Lorica* or *Breastplate,* mentioned as the writing of Gildas in an Irish fifteenth-century collection of religious writings known in Wales as *The Speckled Book*. His authorship, however, has been doubted here by both Mommsen and Williams. Mommsen referred this hymn to the school of writers which produced that strange concoction, the *Hisperica Famina,* though this theory cannot be regarded as proved, in spite of the occurrence of Hisperic words.[89] Williams believed it to be "the work of some unknown writer, who, late in the seventh century, belonged to that South Wales-British circle where Gildas's name was pre-eminent." He held it too complex in its arranging of the angelic host for the time of Gildas, the middle of the sixth century. The editors of the *Irish Liber Hymnorum* thought that it might well be by Gildas, and the question remains unsettled.[90]

The writing falls into three parts, of which the latter two

[89] Mommsen, ed. p. 13; Kennedy, *Sources for the early history of Ireland,* I, p. 271.
[90] Williams, ed. pp. 289ff., with translation on pp. 305ff.: *Irish Lib. Hymn.* I, pp. 206ff.; II, pp. XXIff. (for a discussion of the metre, trochaic trimeter catalectic); pp. 242ff.: *The Book of Cerne,* ed. Dom A. B. Kuypers, pp. 85ff.: Jenkinson, *Hisperica Famina,* pp. XIXff.; 51ff.

are a prayer for the protecting of various portions of the body, related in most careful detail. The first part is more attractive in its appeal to the company of Heaven, described in varying degrees of angels and men. It begins:

> Suffragare trinitatis unitas
> unitatis miserere trinitas;
>
> Suffragare, quaeso, mihi possito
> magni maris velut in periculo,
>
> Ut non secum trahat me mortalitas
> huius anni, neque mundi vanitas.
>
> Et hoc idem peto a sublimibus
> celestis milite virtutibus,
>
> Ne me linquant lacerandum hostibus,
> sed defendant me iam armis fortibus. . . .

Another hymn, assigned to Gildas on good authority, prays for a traveller's protection in journeying by land and sea: against evil spirits, against pirates and robbers, against winds and waves, beasts and serpents, thunder and all deadly weapons of the air; for himself, for his companions, for his money; on ship or on horseback, up mountains and down valleys, through deserts and through forests, till he come to his destined end.[91]

There remain also some fragments from lost letters,[92] remarkable for robust common sense and for a deep spirit of generosity: a refreshing change from bitter censure. All the eight fragments held authentic by Mommsen are marked by this same tone. The first, on excommunication, quotes examples of mercy from the Old Testament, and ends: "Our

---

[91] See W. Meyer, *Nachr. d. Götting. Gesellsch. d. W.: Ph. hist. Kl.* 1912, p. 48ff.; *Poetae Latini aevi Carol.* IV, ed. Strecker, pp. 618f.
[92] Mommsen, ed. pp. 86ff.; Williams, ed. pp. 256ff.; H. and S. I, pp. 108ff.

Lord Jesus Christ did not refuse the feasts of publicans, that He might save all sinners and prostitutes." The second fragment, on abstinence, deserves quotation in full: "Abstinence from bodily food without love is useless. It is better for a man to keep his heart pure in the sight of God, from Whom comes the ending of his life, though he do not fast strictly or refuse over-much the creatures of God, than to hold himself superior to his fellows because he refrains from meat and the delights of worldly food and from riding in carriages or on horseback. To such men as this death has already entered through the windows of their pride."

So in the third fragment: "Many shall perish doing evil, as the Apostle says: 'They have a zeal of God, but not according to knowledge. For they, going about to establish their own righteousness, have not submitted themselves unto the righteousness of God.' " Such men blame all the brethren who have not shared in their presumptuous acts and devices. "They measure out their bread, but boast thereof without measure. They live on water, but are drunken with the wine of hatred. They eat of dry dishes, but revel in slanders. They keep long vigils, but censure others sunk in sleep, saying to the hands and feet of the body: 'If you are not the head, as I am, I shall reckon you naught. . . .' So they prefer fasting to love, vigils to righteousness, their own invention to harmony, a little particular clause to the full doctrine of the Church, austerity to humility, and, last of all, man to God. They heed not the Gospel, but their own will; not the Apostle, but their own pride; forgetting that there are differing degrees of the stars in heaven and differing services of Angels. They fast; but fasting is of no avail if it be not practised for the sake of other virtues."

Better, according to Gildas, to live as a humble inmate of a cloister in reception of sacramental grace than to dare of

spiritual ambition to live unhouselled and unshriven in some
desert far from one's fellowmen.[93] Such admonitions as these
are noteworthy from a monk of the early Celtic Church, renowned for its austerity and its emphasis on mortification of
the flesh.

Equally sound teaching is shown in other fragments of
letters dealing with monks and clergy. Varying degrees of
merit were already recognized in the religious houses of this
time, and, therefore, Gildas advises that a monk from a de-
graded community be readily received into a better one, if
he comes with the right spirit. But only if the community
he leaves is really in a bad way; and if it be remembered
that external appearances make bad standards for judgment:
"We ought not to receive monks against the will of their
Abbot if he himself is not actually excluded for his evil repute
from the table of the blessed. . . . How much more, then,
is it our duty to refuse those who come from holy Abbots,
free from all suspicion of evil, save that they possess cattle
and carriages because of native custom or some infirmity of
their own? Such possessions do less harm to their owners, if
only these be humble and patient, than presumption and
pride do to ploughmen and delvers. Any things of this
world that a monk uses without due necessity should be
counted to him for luxuries and riches; but what he must
use of necessity and not of his own will, lest he should fail
in his work through their lacking, must not be put down to
him as evil."

Humility and charity are the constant theme. "Let the
Chief Priests know that just as the lower clergy must not
despise them, so they must not look down on their clerics,
as the head despising the lower members. . . . Priests and
bishops have a dreadful Judge, and it is for Him, not for

[93] Williams, ed. p. 260.

us, to assess their characters, both in this world and the next.
. . . No one knows the issue of judgment, when we read in
the Scripture of an Apostle lost through greed and of a rob-
ber borne to Paradise on his confession of faith. . . . It is
better that neither fellow-bishops nor fellow-abbots nor fellow-
subjects should criticize each other. If the repute of any
one be unsavoury in his brethren's nostrils, let them in no
wise tell him their thought outright, but rebuke him gently
with patience. So far as conscience permits, let them rather
avoid such men as suspect than excommunicate them as
proved guilty, or banish them from the refectory and the
fellowship of the altar. . . . But let it suffice that a sound
rebuke be administered, because we cannot damn such of-
fenders before the time. They, indeed, may communicate
unworthily. But perhaps we ourselves are holding communion with devils for our evil thoughts. . . . Only for
mortal sins clearly proved, and for no other reason at all,
ought we on necessary occasion to banish brethren from the
fellowship of our altar and our table."

Finally, it is good to quote the last fragment accepted by
Mommsen: "A wise man sees the gleam of truth, no matter
from whose lips it comes."

There is yet one more record of Gildas as monk: his *Penitential,* or list of assessments of penances for divers sins committed by monks, whether priests or deacons or laymen.[94]
Such fixed assessments were part of the discipline exercised
by the early Celtic Church in Britain and in Ireland, from
which their use became general in Europe. Whether such
a "penitence tarifée"[95] was advisable is a matter for experts;
it was of authority for the whole body of monks in the mon-

[94] Williams, ed. pp. 272ff.; H. and S. I., pp. 113ff.; Mommsen, ed.
pp. 89f.
[95] A borrowing from M. Boudinhon: see O. D. Watkins, *History of
Penance,* II, p. 627.

astery for which it was composed, and often, also, for those
who came from the world outside to seek its ministrations
for their guilty souls. It was, therefore, entirely different
from any "list of suggested penances" devised as a possible
aid in the confessional.

We shall return to these Penitentials when we discuss Saint
Columban. For grievous sin Gildas prescribes here the "medicine of penance" of fasting, extending over years apportioned
in careful measure according to the day, Sunday or week-
day, and to the penitent's occupation; also of sleep on a
hard bed and of intensified denial in Lent. Deprivation of
communion accompanied such bodily penance and might be
ordered for as long as a year and a half for deep guilt, though
the offender was allowed to sing the Psalms with his brethren
"lest he lose utterly his soul by so long a time of heavenly
medicine." Tears and hourly petition for forgiveness were
also his means of recovery. Brethren of junior standing and
those obliged to carry on manual work were given lighter
measure of penance. Lesser sins, such as neglect of work,
sudden outbursts of anger, unpunctuality, unpremeditated
irreverence, were also leniently dealt with in comparison with
more serious offences. A brother who could not join in the
Office through drunkenness was deprived of his dinner; one
who broke his rake in gardening was assigned extra work,
"provided it was not broken already." A Priest who made
a slip in saying the Prayer of Consecration at Mass fasted in
penitence three days; for the word DANGER was written
against these holy words to save him from inattention.

And so to preacher and people at a later time Gildas
served to point a moral in time of need. About 793 Alcuin
wrote from Aachen to Ethelheard, Archbishop of Canterbury, in great distress at the invasions of the Northmen into
his native land: "Our fathers, albeit heathen, held this coun-

try under God's providence by their courage in war. What a reproach that we Christians should lose what they gained as heathen? I refer to the scourge which has lately fallen on parts of our island, which our fathers inhabited nearly three hundred and fifty years. We read in the book of Gildas, wisest of Britons, that these same Britons lost their fatherland through the plunderings and the greed of their chieftains, through the iniquity and injustice of their judges, through the sloth and lack of preaching of their bishops, through the self-indulgence and evil manners of their people. Let us see to it that these same offences be not ingrained in our times, that the blessing of God may keep in goodly fortune the fatherland which in His mercy He has designed to give us." **

** *PL* C, 154f.

SELECT BIBLIOGRAPHY

Procopius : *History of the Wars,* Loeb ed. vols. III–V, 1919–1928.

—— *Anecdota (Secret History),* Loeb ed. 1935.

J. B. Bury: *History of the Later Roman Empire,* vols. I and II, 1923.

—— *The Invasion of Europe by the Barbarians,* 1928.

Edward Gibbon: *Decline and Fall of the Roman Empire,* ed. Bury, vols. IV–V, 1909–1911.

T. Hodgkin: *Italy and her Invaders²,* vols. III–VI, 1896–1916.

—— *The Letters of Cassiodorus,* a condensed translation, 1886.

F. Gregorovius: *History of the City of Rome in the Middle Ages⁴,* trans. Hamilton, I, 1900.

Lot-Pfister-Ganshof: *Histoire du Moyen Age,* I, 1928.

H. Grisar: *History of Rome and the Popes in the Middle Ages,* Eng. trans. ed. Cappadelta, vols. II–III, 1912.

F. Lot: *The End of the Ancient World,* trans. Leon, 1931.

W. P. Ker: *The Dark Ages,* 1911.

H. St. L. B. Moss: *The Birth of the Middle Ages,* 1935.

Sir Charles Oman: *The Dark Ages⁶,* 1923.

——*England before the Norman Conquest⁶,* 1924.

W. G. Holmes: *The Age of Justinian and Theodora,* vols. I and II, 1905–1907.

E. K. Rand: *Founders of the Middle Ages²,* 1929.

C. Foligno: *Latin Thought during the Middle Ages,* 1929.

C. C. MIEROW: *The Gothic History of Jordanes,* 1915.

BOETHIUS: *Consolation of Philosophy,* ed. E. K. Rand, with trans. of "I. T." revised by H. F. Stewart, 1926.

—— *The Theological Tractates,* ed. E. K. Rand, trans. Stewart and Rand, 1926.

H. F. STEWART: Boethius: an Essay, 1891.

H. R. PATCH: *The Tradition of Boethius,* 1935.

C. H. HASKINS: *Studies in the History of Mediaeval Science,* 1927.

E. GILSON: *The Spirit of Mediaeval Philosophy,* trans. Downes, 1936.

M. de WULF: *History of Mediaeval Philosophy,* I°, Eng. ed.³, 1935.

H. RASHDALL: *The Universities of Europe in the Middle Ages,* ed. Powicke and Emden, vols. I–III, 1936.

O. M. DALTON: Gregory of Tours: *The History of the Franks,* trans. and commentary, vols. I and II, 1927.

SIR SAMUEL DILL: *Roman Society in Gaul in the Merovingian Age,* 1926.

T. SCOTT HOLMES: *The Origin and Development of the Christian Church in Gaul,* 1911.

D. TARDI: *Fortunat,* 1927.

E. BRIAND: *Histoire de Sainte Radegonde,* 1898.

L. ECKENSTEIN: *Women under Monasticism,* 1896.

F. J. E. RABY: *A History of Christian-Latin Poetry,* 1927.

—— *A History of Secular Latin Poetry in the Middle Ages,* vols. I and II, 1934.

ALBAN BUTLER: *Lives of the Saints,* revised Thurston and Attwater, 1926–1934.

W. J. REES: *Lives of the Cambro-British Saints,* 1853.

H. WILLIAMS: ed. and trans. *Works* of Gildas, 1899.

—— *Christianity in Early Britain,* 1912.

SELECT BIBLIOGRAPHY

J. E. Lloyd: *A History of Wales*, I, 1911.

Eugippius: *Life of Saint Severinus*, trans. G. W. Robinson, 1914.

C. F. Arnold: *Caesarius von Arelate*, 1894.

A. Malnory: *Saint Césaire*, 1894.

Baring-Gould and Fisher: *Lives of the British Saints*, vols. I–IV, 1907.

Count de Montalembert: *The Monks of the West*, vols. I–III, 1896.

Adamnan: *Life of St. Columba*, ed. W. Reeves², 1874.

Jonas: *Life of St. Columban*, Univ. Pennsylvania, *Translations and Reprints*, II, 1902, No. 7.

J. A. Duke: *The Columban Church*, 1932.

—— *History of the Church in Scotland*, 1937.

Louis Gougaud: *Christianity in Celtic Lands*, trans. Joynt, 1932.

J. F. Kenney: *Sources for the Early History of Ireland*, I, 1929.

W. A. Phillips: ed. *History of the Church of Ireland*, I, 1933.

John Ryan: *Irish Monasticism*, 1931.

W. K. Lowther Clarke: *The Rule of St. Benedict*, 1931.

Paul Delatte: *Commentary on the Rule of St. Benedict*, 1921.

F. Cabrol: *Saint Benedict*, trans. Antony, 1934.

Cuthbert Butler: *Benedictine Monachism*², 1924.

E. G. Gardner: ed. *The Dialogues of Saint Gregory*, translation of ann. 1608.

Gregory the Great: *The Pastoral Rule*, trans. Bramley, 1874. *Pastoral Rule*; Selected *Letters*, trans. Barmby, *Nicene and Post-Nicene Fathers*, XII, *Morals on the*

Book of Job, trans. *Library of the Fathers*, vols. I–III, 1844-1847.

G. F. BROWNE : *King Alfred's Books*, 1920.

F. HOMES DUDDEN : *Gregory the Great*, vols. I and II, 1905.

P. BATIFFOL : *Saint Gregory the Great*, trans. Stoddard, 1929.

INDEX

SELECTED ANN ARBOR PAPERBACKS

works of enduring merit

For a complete list of Ann Arbor Paperback titles write:

THE UNIVERSITY OF MICHIGAN PRESS / ANN ARBOR